As one of the world's longest established
and best-known travel brands,
Thomas Cook are the experts in travel.

For more than 135 years our
guidebooks have unlocked the secrets
of destinations around the world,
sharing with travellers a wealth of
experience and a passion for travel.

**Rely on Thomas Cook as your
travelling companion on your next trip
and benefit from our unique heritage.**

r guides

FLORIDA
Ryan Levitt with Jason R Rich

Your travelling companion since 1873

Thomas
Cook

Written by Ryan Levitt with Jason R Rich, updated by Jason R Rich
Original photography by Jason Clampet

Published by Thomas Cook Publishing
A division of Thomas Cook Tour Operations Limited.
Company registration no. 3772199 England
The Thomas Cook Business Park, Unit 9, Coningsby Road,
Peterborough PE3 8SB, United Kingdom
Email: books@thomascook.com, Tel: + 44 (0) 1733 416477
www.thomascookpublishing.com

Produced by Cambridge Publishing Management Limited
Burr Elm Court, Main Street, Caldecote CB23 7NU

ISBN: 978-1-84848-213-5

First edition © 2008 Thomas Cook Publishing
This second edition © 2009
Text © Thomas Cook Publishing
Maps © Thomas Cook Publishing/PCGraphics (UK) Limited

Series Editor: Maisie Fitzpatrick
Production/DTP: Steven Collins

Printed and bound in Italy by Printer Trento

Cover photography: © FRANCES Stéphane/hemis.fr

Contents

Introduction

Why come to Florida on holiday? It's almost an impossible question to answer because there are so many reasons to rush out and book! Blessed by natural beauty, bathed in sunshine, home to the country's most popular theme parks and easily accessible, it is America's East Coast playground – and has been for over a century.

Surrounded by water, Florida is seemingly an endless line of beaches, each with its own characteristics and attractions. Looking for quiet solitude and powder-soft sand? Then it's the Panhandle for you! Want sizzling nightlife and café culture? South Beach is the place to head for. Or if you're a bohemian spirit, why not head over to America's southernmost point, Key West?

Families adore Florida because there really is something in the state to appeal to every member of the family. People of all ages, especially children and teenagers, adore the theme parks in Orlando, tots can play on the sandy beaches or explore the various children's museums, while parents can escape on the boardwalks of the Gulf Coast to appreciate the sunsets. Tourism is a major industry in this state and tour operators are now offering incredible value and flexibility in their packages. Gone are the days when you had to choose between either a seven- or a four-night stay. Now you can pick a

duration that suits your needs. You can even make it a two- or three-centre stay to see more of the state.

Many people feel they have done Florida after a single visit to Miami or Orlando. To think this is to make a very grave mistake indeed. Florida boasts a number of diverse regions that beg for multiple visits. Sports lovers can charter boats off the coast, tee off at world-class championship courses, hike through old-growth forests or take a spin on a powerboat along the borders of the Everglades. Those looking for an indulgent break will be drawn to the collection of elite resorts operated by some of the world's most luxurious hotel chains. Sample the spa menus, shop for designer goods or show off your bling at a salsa lesson – no matter what your preference, it's all here for you.

Florida is a bit like the most popular person in school: difficult to approach, but once you do, welcoming and friendly forever more. Marketing campaigns may draw your attention to vast amusement parks and holiday complexes, but there is so much more to see and do than visit the house that a mouse built.

For those who say America has no history, go and explore St Augustine, America's oldest mainland port. In December, candlelight processions light up the town in preparation for Christmas celebrations. It's truly a magical moment.

Gay and lesbian travellers will appreciate the hassle-free welcome they receive at resorts across the state, so if you're with your partner, feel free to ask for a double room without compromise. The Walt Disney World® Resort even hosts unofficial, and extremely successful, annual 'Gay Days' events, which attract thousands from the LGBT community (*www.gaydays.com*).

The key to getting the most out of Florida is to expand your horizons. Choose the popular resorts, yes, but be sure to get out and explore the parts of the state that you might not have heard of before, for these hidden jewels are Florida's best-kept secret.

Introduction

Sanibel Beach, near Sanibel Lighthouse

The state

They say that Florida would be the first piece of land to go if ever global warming melted the icecaps. Flat as a pancake, with portions of the land actually below sea level, it's a pretty homogeneous place. Or is it? Look beyond the surface and you'll find hundreds of micro-environments such as coral reefs, sandy beaches and mangrove forests forming regions ripe for exploration. You may not find purple-mountain majesty, but you'll certainly understand what makes Florida attractive to so many visitors.

Florida is America's southernmost mainland state, looking something like a big comma hanging down from the Southern States. Surrounding it on three sides is water, a geographic blessing that has transformed it into America's holiday paradise. No matter where you are in Florida, you'll never be more than a three-hour drive from the coast. At its highest point, the state lies a mere 350ft (107m) above sea level, with south Florida the lowest point of all.

Miami and the south Atlantic

Florida's most famous city, Miami, lies at the southeast tip of the mainland. This part of the state is the most developed and populous with communities lining the coast all the way up the Atlantic. Land reclamation has allowed Miami to sprawl, but it has also put the population a little closer to wildlife than it might like with the Everglades National Park lapping at its borders. It is not uncommon for crocodiles to wander out of the park and into the back gardens of Miami's western suburbs.

Lying just off the coast of Miami and linked by a causeway is Miami Beach, home to South Beach and thousands of decadent residents. Golden sand beaches are caressed by the waves at this popular resort, but erosion is occurring and sand is regularly trucked in. Key Biscayne, a secluded island off the coast of Miami, offers great nature trails, or go west from Miami to explore the mangrove forests, swamps and ancient wildlife that call the Everglades home. Here, you will find Florida's greatest conglomeration of protected species, including abundant birdlife.

The Florida Keys

From Miami, head southwest along US 1 to reach the coral islands that lie like pearls scattered in a line along the ocean. Key Largo is the entry point for the keys, but you might not want to stay too long in this touristy town.

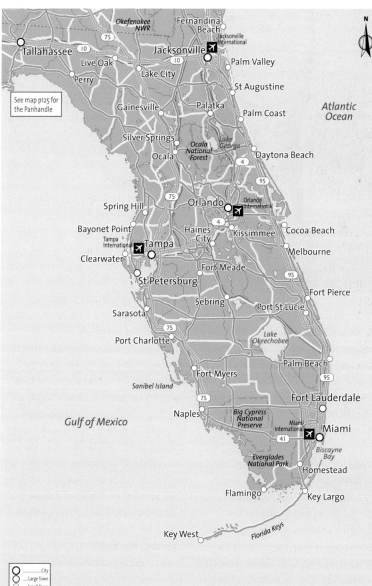

The state

Okefenokee NWR

Fernandina Beach

Tallahassee

Jacksonville International

Jacksonville

Palm Valley

Live Oak

Lake City

St Augustine

Perry

See map p125 for the Panhandle

Gainesville

Palatka

Palm Coast

Atlantic Ocean

Silver Springs

Lake George

Ocala National Forest

Ocala

Daytona Beach

Spring Hill

Orlando

Orlando International

Bayonet Point

Haines City

Kissimmee

Cocoa Beach

Tampa International

Tampa

Clearwater

Melbourne

St Petersburg

Fort Meade

Sebring

Fort Pierce

Sarasota

Port St Lucie

Port Charlotte

Lake Okeechobee

Fort Myers

Palm Beach

Sanibel Island

Gulf of Mexico

Naples

Big Cypress National Preserve

Fort Lauderdale

Miami International

Miami

Biscayne Bay

Everglades National Park

Homestead

Flamingo

Key Largo

Key West

Florida Keys

........City
........Large Town
........Small Town
........Motorway
........Main Road
........Minor Road
........Airport
........Railway

0   100km

0   50 miles

A public park in Palm Beach

Instead, keep driving for over two hours along the route until you get to the end of the line: Key West. The drive to reach Key West is one of the most attractive in the state, passing along causeways over the Straits of Florida. Coral reefs line the southern coast of the Keys, making underwater diving a wonderful option. The islands, too, are coral, having risen over the sea level over time. As such, they house numerous species of unique flora and fauna native only to this region of the state.

Tampa and the Gulf Coast resorts

Tampa lies at the end of Tampa Bay, protected from the Gulf of Mexico by a jut of land that houses St Petersburg and Clearwater. A series of islands lines the west coast of the Pinellas Peninsula,

offering fantastic birding, beaches and mangrove forests. Further north is the Crystal River, where manatees often frolic due to the warmer waters.

To the south, a chain of barrier islands continues to stretch as far as Sarasota. Resorts along this stretch offer white-sand beaches and fantastic shell-collecting, especially on Sanibel Island.

The northeast

When NASA took over Cape Canaveral, they took too much land for their requirements. What they didn't use, they have since turned into a bird sanctuary and National Wildlife Refuge. The Canaveral National Seashore is now a 13-mile (21km) stretch of barrier islands lined with beaches filled with cabbage palms, marshes, sea grapes, palmettos and lagoons. Inside, you can spot ibises, egrets, terns and sanderlings. To the southwest you can also visit the Merritt Island National Wildlife Refuge, which is home to alligators, waterfowl and reptiles, many endangered. Continue north to the industrial city of Jacksonville before heading towards the Georgia border for the Victorian-era resort of Amelia Island, once the holiday destination of choice for America's black population.

Thanks to the Walt Disney World® Resort, Universal Orlando and SeaWorld® theme parks and resorts, Orlando has been the most popular tourist destination in the United States for several decades. Every year, millions come to Orlando to experience the rides, shows and attractions that only the theme parks can provide. Located close to these popular parks are also dozens of smaller, family-friendly attractions and activities.

The Panhandle

For the best beaches in Florida, head to the Panhandle. Pale-white beaches, small crowds and crystal-blue waters are the hallmarks of the region, made beautiful by the quartz particles that have eroded for centuries down from the Appalachian Mountains in order to create the grains of sand you see today. The Gulf Islands National Seashore protects over 100 miles (160km) of these beaches, keeping the coast pristine. Inland is where you will finally see some rolling hills, especially in and around the city of Tallahassee. Old-growth forests lie near the capital, perfect for hiking and canoeing. Even driving here is enjoyable: ancient oaks covered in Spanish moss have grown so close together that they have formed canopies over the roads.

Sun-seekers from across the South flock to the beach at Panama City

The state

History

12,000 BC	Diverse groups of Native Americans begin to inhabit Florida.
1513	Ponce de León claims Florida during his search for the Fountain of Youth.
1763	Britain gets control of Florida in return for Havana.
1783	Spain once more flies its flag on Floridian soil following the Second Treaty of Paris.
1814	America makes periodic raids into Florida claiming they are looking for runaway slaves from Georgia.
1817–19	Seminoles become legendary for their bravery and battle techniques during the First Seminole War.
1818	Andrew Jackson takes Pensacola from the Spanish.
1819	The Spanish cede Florida to the upstart Americans, unable to guarantee the region's safety any longer.
1835–42	The Second Seminole War rages after America attempts to force the Seminoles to live in barren lands west of the Mississippi River. Some Seminoles escape to the Everglades, where their descendants remain.
1845	Florida becomes a full state after it joins the Union.
1848	Miami is founded.
1855–58	The Third Seminole War.
1860	Abraham Lincoln is elected, resulting in Civil War. Florida joins the Confederates.
1868	Florida rejoins the Union.
1896	Henry Flagler completes his railway. Miami is granted city status shortly thereafter.
1921	George Merrick builds the city of Coral Gables.
1929	Florida enters the Great Depression following the Stock Market crash.
1930s	The era of Art Deco: Miami Beach becomes the holiday place of choice

	for wealthy Yankees. Dozens of hotels are built to meet demand.
1935	400 die following a massive hurricane that hits the state.
1941	America joins World War II, transforming Pensacola and Miami into important naval bases.
1947	Everglades National Park is created.
1958	Cape Canaveral launches its first rocket into space.
1959	The Cuban revolution forces thousands of Cubans to flee to Miami.
1961	The disastrous Bay of Pigs invasion. Many are killed.
1962	The Cuban Missile Crisis brings America to the brink of war.
1964	Walt Disney begins buying land near Orlando.
1971	The Walt Disney World® Resort opens. Epcot® was added in 1982, Disney's Hollywood Studios™ in 1989 and Disney's Animal Kingdom® in 1998.
1973	SeaWorld® Orlando opens.
1980	The Mariel Boatlift brings hundreds of Cuba's unwanted to Miami after Castro lets them go freely.
1986	The *Challenger* space shuttle explodes, killing seven crew.
1990	Universal Orlando opens.
1992	Hurricane Andrew hits.
1996	Miami turns 100 years old.
1997	Gianni Versace is killed at his South Beach home.
2000	Bush gains the presidency after Florida's vote is declared in his favour.
2004	Bush wins again while his brother celebrates as Governor.
2008	Barack Obama wins Florida with nearly 51 per cent of the vote, and becomes the 44th President of the United States.
2010	After becoming the most keenly anticipated theme park attraction in history, The Wizarding World of Harry Potter opens at Universal Orlando.

Politics and media

For years, Florida was a Democrat stronghold that swung in the direction of the party in every election. However, as immigration to the state has exploded, retirees have purchased property and cold Yankees have decided that they no longer want to deal with snow, demographics have changed.

Today, the state is evenly split right down party lines, with south Florida counties like Miami-Dade and Fort Lauderdale-Broward County sticking with the Democrats, and the north mainly Republican. Friction is often a problem as both parties consider Florida to be a battleground state with numerous electoral votes worth fighting over.

The most important political event of this century occurred in 2000 when Florida went Republican in one of the most controversial votes ever. Florida's 'hanging chad' fiasco, whereby individual ballots were hand-counted one-by-one, resulted in the selection of George W Bush as the President of the United States, with Democrats screaming that the man had stolen the election. The difference was the closest margin in American history, causing the state to become highly polarised. America still talks about how Florida stole the presidency from Gore (or saved it from him – depending on

which party is talking). The vote in 2008 was remarkably close again, with Barack Obama just edging out John McCain by 50.9 per cent to 48.4 per cent.

The state capital is located in Tallahassee, a sleepy southern city near the Georgia border. Residing in the capital is the Governor, who is responsible for representing the state at a national level and determining the best course of action for its residents.

Shifts in voting patterns among the Cuban population have come following a number of perceived blunders made by the Clinton team during their time in the White House. Kennedy put forth the Bay of Pigs plan to retake Cuba and Cubans loved him for it. Clinton made efforts to re-establish ties with Cuba and the Democrat party soon became the party of last resort among the vast Cuban-American population. However, Obama did well with Latino voters in 2008.

Reporting on all these political foibles is the local press. Unlike the UK,

Florida (and the United States) does not house a respected national media that covers hard news. Local news is where it's at, meaning that if you switch on the television at the news hour, you'll see local events showcased rather than global issues.

The first newspapers began publishing in Florida in 1780, and if locals from that period fast-forwarded to modern times, they'd see that little has changed as coverage continues to be focused on the needs and interests of Spanish-speaking islands and communities. Today, the big three in the state are the *Miami Herald*, the *Orlando Sentinel* and the *St Petersburg Times*. The *Tallahassee Democrat* is also a good bet if local politics interests you in any way.

Television stations are franchises of larger networks. All of the big five (ABC, CBS, CW, Fox, NBC) have stations across the state. In fact, The Walt Disney Company owns the ABC network, along with several popular nationwide cable TV stations.

The Old State Capitol building in Tallahassee

Culture

A diverse population means that culture is alive and well in Florida. The state has drawn artists and their patrons from across the country for generations, all enticed by its balmy shores and bohemian lifestyles. Whether it's visual arts, performance, architecture or history that you find fascinating, Florida will have the space or gallery to startle and entertain. You might not think of ever leaving the beach, but you'd be missing out on world-class options and exhilarating performances if you didn't.

Art

There are many art galleries of world renown that call Florida home. By far the most notable is St Petersburg's Salvador Dalí Museum, which houses the largest collection of works by the great Surrealist anywhere on the planet. The Miami Art Museum is a new addition to Florida's cultural community, putting its focus on family-friendly exhibitions, making it a great place to head for if you want to expose your children to visual arts in a fun and informative manner. Modern masterpieces can be found at Fort Lauderdale's Museum of Art, which boasts wonderful works from Warhol, Dalí and Moore in its collection. If you're looking to buy rather than view, the shops of Palm Beach, Key West, Naples and Sarasota are scattered with independent galleries featuring the work of local artists.

Theatre

Few plays have actually been set in Florida; however, the state has a thriving collection of performance spaces dotted across the region. In fact, Florida State University has consistently been ranked as one of the top ten schools for theatre in the country for a number of years. Hundreds of theatre professionals have graduated from this leading institution, ending up on the stages of Broadway and beyond.

Fort Lauderdale Museum of Art

Culture

The Coconut Grove Playhouse is a good regional theatre

Almost all large towns in Florida boast a multipurpose performing arts space. However, these theatres usually only programme large-scale bus-and-truck touring productions taken straight from Broadway. So, if you want to see a big-budget musical or hit play, these are the places to head for. Examples include the César Pelli-designed Miami Performing Arts Center and the Tampa Bay Performing Arts Center.

Florida also has a vibrant collection of regional theatre, some of which can boast national recognition. Productions here are commercial, yet slightly edgier. Think off-Broadway inventiveness rather than Broadway dazzle and glitz. The Coconut Grove Playhouse in Coconut Grove and GableStage in Coral Gables are two such options.

Repertory theatre is on display at the jewel-like Asolo Theatre in Sarasota, a transplanted opera house that was brought over to Florida from Italy by John Ringling.

Universal Orlando's CityWalk has become the permanent home of the off-Broadway hit Blue Man Group, while the Walt Disney World® Resort is where you'll find Cirque du Soleil: *La Nouba*, an original show created by the French-Canadian circus troupe that has become very popular worldwide.

Cinema

The list of films shot in Florida is truly endless. Almost year-round sun means long shooting days for expensive crews. Heat and humidity provide incredible atmosphere for film noir, crime and action thrillers, and the choice of

Hemingway's house in Key West

communities, including swanky resort towns and backwater country, means that you can shoot almost any story within the state's borders.

The first movie to have an effect on Florida's tourism was *Key Largo*, the classic noir thriller featuring the smoky sexiness of Humphrey Bogart and Lauren Bacall. It was so popular that the town known today as Key Largo changed its name from Rock Harbor, to match the name of the film.

Following its success, other filmmakers decided to use Florida as a backdrop, with the next blockbuster coming in the Marilyn Monroe vehicle *Some Like It Hot*, where Jack Lemmon and Tony Curtis hide out from the mob by joining an all-girl band. Ironically, neither *Some Like It Hot* nor *Key Largo* was ever filmed in the state.

More recent blockbusters have put Florida firmly on the map, including *Scarface*, *True Lies* (with Jamie Lee Curtis holding on for dear life from a helicopter over US 1 along the Keys), *Get Shorty* and *Miami Vice.*

Literature

Florida has spawned a number of authors and works throughout its history. Warm climates offer respite and relaxation for the creative mind, and no author has been drawn to its bounty more than Ernest Hemingway. The legendary 'man's man' lived in Key West from 1931 to 1940. His classic work *To Have and Have Not* was written during his time in the town.

Contemporary authors have also flourished, with big names such as Carl Hiaasen and Elmore Leonard setting many of their most important works in the state. Both writers were former reporters with the *Miami Herald* and their work reflects the sarcasm prevalent when dealing with Florida's mixed-up political and mafia scenes.

In fact, crime thrillers seem to thrive in Miami as the region's mix of sin, sand and sun provides colourful backdrops and plenty of atmosphere. *Miami Blues* by Charles Willeford is one of the most popular examples of this genre.

African-American literature has also found Florida to be a strong setting. Zora Neale Hurston's seminal work *Their Eyes Were Watching God* portrays the life of a strong black woman as she faces trials and tribulations in Florida's countryside.

Folklore and legends

According to popular legend, Florida was discovered by Juan Ponce de León when he was searching for the Fountain of Youth. Commissioned by the Spanish crown to discover new lands, his fleet landed near modern-day St Augustine and created America's first permanent European settlement. Ponce de León didn't discover the spring, but he did establish Florida as a Spanish territory, setting in motion the chain of events that led the state to join the Union in 1845.

It took a long time for Florida to establish itself as an economic powerhouse of any form, primarily due to the inhospitable topography of much of the state. Swamps in the south, deep mangrove forests and offshore coral reefs exacted a lot of damage on early settlers. In fact, sailors believed that the Florida manatees were actually mermaids drawing ships to their death through their song. If you look at a manatee today, you might wonder just exactly what the sailors of yesteryear were drinking during their long voyages.

Finally, Cuban influence arrived after the revolution, bringing with the immigrants the Santería religion. Practitioners can be consulted about the future should you be interested in appeasing the many gods that exist in their stories and ceremonies.

Culture

The entrance to the Fountain of Youth, St Augustine

Festivals and events

A multitude of cultures, fantastic weather and a love of all things Americana means that there's almost always something to do in Florida. As the state with both America's oldest town and its widest range of theme parks and attractions, you can choose from events that feature a historic twist like the candlelight processions through the town of St Augustine or those that are built purely for enjoyment, like the racing in Daytona. Take it slow or speed it up by looking at the following festival and event options.

January

Orange Bowl Football Game College football is huge in Florida, and this championship is what they all play for. Held in Miami every January. (*Usually 1 January.*)
Tel: (305) 341 4700. www.orangebowl.org
Walt Disney World® Marathon An annual race through the Disney theme parks that attracts thousands.
http://disneyworldsports.disney.go.com

February

Miami International Film Festival This film festival hosted by Miami-Dade College is particularly good at showing documentaries that wouldn't see the light of day in your average Cineplex. (*Usually begins last week of February.*)
Tel: (305) 405 6433.
www.miamifilmfestival.com
Speedweeks Enjoy a week of top stock-car racing, culminating in the running of the annual Daytona 500. (*Begins second week of February.*)

Tel: (386) 254 2700.
www.daytonaintlspeedway.com

March

Carnaval Miami Celebrate Latin culture during this annual week-long festival that features Latin music performances, salsa dancing, live bands and beauty contests. (*Begins first Friday in March.*)
Tel: (305) 644 8888.
www.carnavalmiami.com
Epcot® International Flower Show and Garden Festival Interactive and breathtaking gardens are showcased at this annual event. (*Until June.*)
http://disneyworld.disney.go.com/ special-events
Spring Break Thousands of college kids from across North America converge on Daytona Beach, Key West and Panama City Beach. (*Schedules dependent on college terms, usually second and third weeks of the month.*)
Winter Music Conference This annual conference of DJs, musicians and

promoters is so influential that BBC Radio One has been known to broadcast live from the event, held at venues throughout Miami. (*Usually last week of March.*) *Tel: (954) 563 4444. www.wmcon.com*

April

Billboard Latin Music Awards See your favourite Latin performers at this annual awards ceremony in Miami. (*Usually first weekend of April.*) *Tel: (646) 654 4660. www.billboardevents.com*

PGA Seniors Golf Tournament Boca Raton hosts this annual golf tournament, the most prestigious of all on the senior circuit. (*Dates alter annually – call for updates.*) *Tel: (561) 624 8400. www.pga.com*

July

Blue Angels Air Show See navy pilots do dazzling tricks in the skies above Pensacola. (*Usually third weekend of July.*) *Tel: (850) 434 1234. www.blueangels.navy.mil*

September

Epcot® International Food and Wine Festival Adult theme park guests can sample exotic wines and taste food prepared by world-class visiting chefs. Live cooking demonstrations, music and seminars. (*Until November.*) *http://disneyworld.disney.go.com/special-events*

Labor Day Pro-Am Surfing Festival An annual event in Cocoa Beach that brings in amateurs and pros. (*First Monday in September.*) *Tel: (321) 459 2200. www.space-coast.com*

November

American Sandsculpting Festival Your castle will never look as good as the creations on Fort Myers Beach. (*First weekend of November.*) *Tel: (239) 454 7500. www.fortmyersbeach.org*

The Osborne Family Spectacle of Dancing Lights The backlot area of Disney's Hollywood Studios™ is transformed into a winter wonderland, complete with man-made snow. (*Mid-November until early January.*) *http://disneyworld.disney.go.com/special-events*

White Party The biggest gay circuit party of them all, drawing over 15,000 people to Miami. (*Last weekend of November.*) *Tel: (305) 576 1234. www.whiteparty.org*

December

Art Basel Miami Beach Over 150 galleries host this annual art fair. (*First weekend of December.*) *Tel: (305) 674 1292.*

British Night Watch and Grand Illumination Ceremony Join a procession in St Augustine to start the Christmas celebrations. (*First Saturday in December.*) *www.getaway4florida.com*

Highlights

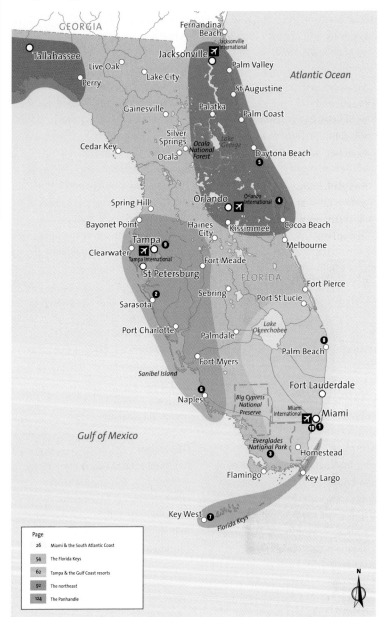

GEORGIA

Fernandina Beach

Tallahassee

Live Oak

Lake City

Perry

Jacksonville
Jacksonville International

Palm Valley

Atlantic Ocean

St Augustine

Gainesville

Palatka

Palm Coast

Silver Springs

Cedar Key

Ocala National Forest

Lake George

Ocala

Daytona Beach ❺

Spring Hill

Orlando
Orlando International ❹

Bayonet Point

Haines City

Kissimmee

Cocoa Beach

Tampa ❸
Tampa International

Clearwater

Fort Meade

Melbourne

St Petersburg

FLORIDA

❷

Sebring

Fort Pierce

Sarasota

Port St Lucie

Port Charlotte

Lake Okeechobee

Palmdale

Palm Beach ❽

Fort Myers

Sanibel Island

Fort Lauderdale

Naples ❻

Big Cypress National Preserve

Miami International

Miami
❿ ❶

Gulf of Mexico

Everglades National Park ❾

Homestead

Flamingo

Key Largo

Key West ❼

Florida Keys

N

❶ Art Deco architecture of South Beach South Beach came into its own during the 1930s. Today, the Art Deco architecture looks better than ever (*see pp36–7*).

❷ Sarasota's art scene Ringling built the circus, but he was also an art connoisseur. Upon his death, he willed hundreds of treasures to the town (*see p78*).

❸ Everglades adventures Crocs and gators and swamps. Visit Florida's most famous national park (*see pp140–41*).

Art Deco-style hotel on Miami's Ocean Drive

❹ Watching a NASA shuttle blast-off Reach for the stars in Cape Canaveral and see how far the power of dreams can take us (*see pp94–5*).

❺ Racing at Daytona Visit in February to watch the Daytona 500, one of the most popular races in the world of motor sports (*see pp96–7*).

❻ The beaches of Naples Watch the sunset from the pristine beaches of Naples, considered the swankiest resort on the Gulf Coast (*see pp90–91*).

❼ Driving US 1 along the Keys From Key West to Miami, US 1 takes you along Florida's most delicious coast lined with coral and cosy communities (*see pp56–7*).

❽ Worth Avenue shopping and luxury in Palm Beach Chanel, Hermès and all labels in between (*see p51*).

❾ Roller coasters at Busch Gardens Loop-the-loop, drop 60ft (18m) in a second, or roar along at 50mph (80km/h) (*see pp66–7*).

❿ Walt Disney World® Resort The 4 theme parks, 2 water parks, 5 golf courses and 33 resort hotels are just some of the attractions at America's top tourist destination (*see pp112–18*). Nearby are Universal Orlando (*see pp118–21*) and SeaWorld® (*see pp121–3*).

Highlights

Suggested itineraries

Long weekend

Jet into Miami and live a life of luxury on South Beach. By day, explore the Art Deco architecture of the resort and tan yourself on the golden sands of Florida's most famous stretch of sand. By night, party on Collins Avenue with the beautiful people, making sure to grab a cup of coffee at the News Café when you want a break from the action.

Once you've tired of the South Beach scene, go to the mainland where you can immerse yourself in Cuban culture in Little Havana. Get your fortune told at a Santería shop or take salsa dance lessons at one of the local clubs. Sporting types should try to snag

SheiKra roller coaster, Busch Gardens

tickets to see one of the professional sports teams in action. If you've never seen American football, the Miami Dolphins are a great team to watch, even if they have been on a losing streak over the past few seasons. Alternatively, if shopping is your exercise, head over to Fort Lauderdale's Sawgrass Mills shopping centre for outlet bargains. High-end designer duds can be seen at the Shops at Bal Harbour if you don't want to make the trek.

Culture vultures won't want to miss heading over to Coconut Grove and Coral Gables where world-class theatre is available at the Coconut Grove Playhouse and The Gables. End your stay by taking a day trip out to the Everglades to see Florida's abundant wildlife, including alligators! By this time you should be ready to check back in for your flight home.

A long weekend in Orlando is barely enough time to visit the Walt Disney World® Resort, Universal Orlando or SeaWorld®. Plan on spending one to two full days per theme park, so pick the type of experience you want most. Don't even try to see and do everything!

One week

An extended stay of one week is a great period of time to explore the wonders of the Gulf Coast. Head to Tampa as your first stop and budget at least a day to experience Busch Gardens, Florida's theme park of choice for roller coasters and animal encounters. Keep your fire burning at night in Ybor City, a neighbourhood in Tampa that once housed a wide array of cigar factories that have since been transformed into sizzle-hot nightclubs and bars. Pop up to Clearwater after you have exhausted your adrenalin to flop onto the beaches of this popular resort.

Head south along the coast, making sure to swing by Solomon's Castle near Bradenton for an intriguing look at what one man can do with the trash of others. The home he has built from used materials is an inspiring sight.

Next stop is Sarasota, a location known for its artistic offerings. If you can get tickets to a performance at the Asolo Theatre, then be sure to go for it. Even if the production is poor (which it rarely is), a view of the interior is worth the cost of admission alone. Other highlights in this elegant community are boardwalk strolls and a stop at the Circus Museum to see how Ringling made the fortune that transformed the community.

If you're making good time, continue along the coast to Fort Myers to see the former retreat of Thomas Edison and then continue on to Naples, considered to be the Gulf Coast's version of Palm Beach.

In a week, visitors can get a taste of the Orlando-area theme parks. You could easily spend the entire time at the Walt Disney World® Resort, or take the opportunity to visit the parks at Universal Orlando and/or SeaWorld® as

Street sculpture in Sarasota

well. Plan on spending one to two full days per theme park to truly experience it and get your money's worth. The activities and attractions along International Drive offer a diversion from the theme parks, while Downtown Orlando offers more cultural activities such as theatre and museums.

Two weeks

Start your trip in Tampa, being sure to visit Busch Gardens, Ybor City and the renowned Salvador Dalí Museum in St Petersburg. If you need to cool off, Adventure Island provides plenty of diversions for the whole family. The Florida Aquarium is the best of its kind in Florida, if not the country. An afternoon here is well spent and may spark your desire to head up to the Crystal River to see manatees frolic in their native habitat. Take a break from

Fort Lauderdale

this hectic schedule with a day on the beaches in Clearwater, where you'll find relaxing nooks and busy stretches within yards of each other along the coastline.

From here, it's a trip down south to see the sights of Sarasota and Bradenton before ending up in Fort Myers, an enjoyable resort catering to those looking for a quiet corner of paradise. After you've seen your share of the region, take the ferry down to bohemian Key West. Spend a few days exploring mainland America's southernmost point, filling your days with deep-sea fishing trips and strolls through the character-filled streets and your nights drinking on Duval Street.

From here, take a drive up US 1 towards Key Largo, being sure to make stops in the communities along the way. Diving and kayaking are great along the Keys, so spend a day exploring above or below the waterline. Zip through Key Largo until you reach Miami where your holiday ends on South Beach with a chilled cocktail as you watch the sun rise over the Atlantic.

Spending a full week at the Walt Disney World® Resort, followed by a few days at Universal Orlando or SeaWorld®, will give you a good feel for the area's theme parks. Also, take a day trip to nearby Cape Canaveral and Cocoa Beach, Tampa and/or Daytona Beach. Aside from the theme parks, you'll find plenty of museums, cultural activities, and outdoor adventures (such as airboat or hot air balloon rides) that can make any holiday memorable. Golf, horse-riding, fishing, boating and hiking are readily available as half-day or full-day activities.

Longer

Follow the itinerary listed above for a two-week journey until you reach Miami. Spend a few days exploring Miami and South Beach, making sure to venture beyond the beach to enjoy the city's diversity. If you have the time, incorporate a day trip to the Everglades by taking a quick drive along the Tamiami Trail.

Go north from Miami towards Fort Lauderdale where you can charter a boat for a trip around the town's canals and waterways. Shop till you drop at Sawgrass Mills and then continue on the road until you reach Palm Beach. Live the life of luxury for a few days, showing off your tan, labels and jewellery. A walk up Worth Avenue is a must, if only to see how the other half lives.

Continue your trip to Cocoa Beach and Cape Canaveral. If you time it right, you may spot a space shuttle launch, but even if you don't, a visit to the Kennedy Space Center is a must. Feeling daring? Learn to surf on Cocoa Beach or go for a spin at the Daytona Speedway. You can even rent a dune buggy for a jaunt along Daytona's coast to join the teens and college kids on their spring break.

Don't stop now! Cut northwest across to the Panhandle and Tallahassee, Florida's capital. Explore the canopy roads that ring the city or test yourself with a hike along the 30-mile (48km) trail that runs through Apalachicola National Forest. Then end your stay partying it up in Pensacola and Panama City where you can say 'I've seen Florida'.

With a rental car, it is easy to explore large areas of Florida with relative ease. One or two weeks can offer you a very thorough exploration of the area's theme parks, and also allow you to take full advantage of your resort's amenities. You can also consider one- to three-day trips to other popular Florida cities and destinations that offer vastly different holiday experiences – Cocoa Beach, Palm Beach, Miami, Fort Lauderdale, the Florida Keys, Sarasota and Clearwater.

Incredible dining, nightlife, shopping and Latin culture can be found in Miami, for example, while Sarasota is where you'll discover some of the most spectacular and beautiful beaches in all of the USA. Palm Beach and Boca Raton are like the Beverly Hills of Florida, while the Florida Keys offer beaches and resorts where relaxing in the sun is the most popular activity.

Driving along Daytona Beach

Miami and the South Atlantic Coast

Florida has long been a desired holiday destination – and this stretch of sand is where it all began. The passion of local residents to make south Florida the destination of choice for moneyed northerners is what transformed the fortunes of the region, eventually drawing Standard Oil millionaire Henry Morrison to build a number of five-star hotels and a railway along Florida's Atlantic Coast.

A boom during the 1930s built up the region's fortunes (and architectural legacy), only for the 1970s and 1980s to bring a period of decline, high crime and neglect.

Many consider Madonna to be the person responsible for the resurgence of Miami Beach as a holiday option. Her presence in the early 1990s brought dozens of celebrities down to the south Atlantic shores and revitalised the entire coast. Today, the Art Deco architecture is fresher than ever and the entire region looks more beautiful than it ever did.

First-timers will probably want to base themselves at South Beach, located on the tip of a peninsula linked by a causeway to Downtown. The Downtown core is also experiencing a bit of a revival thanks to a number of new arts and sporting developments. To the immediate west of Downtown lies Little Havana – heart of the Latin community. Or go southwest from here for the more sedate holiday communities of Coconut Grove and Coral Gables. Key Biscayne, the exclusive retreat for a number of celebrities, lies across a causeway to the southeast of Downtown. Get away from Miami by going north along either the A1A or I-95. Both roads pass through Palm Beach, passing through sunspots like Fort Lauderdale and Boca Raton and eventually ending up at Jupiter Island.

MIAMI
Downtown

For many years, Downtown Miami was a place to avoid – an abandoned network of discount shops populated by the down-and-out members of the local Hispanic communities. A mere decade ago, historic buildings, once shining beacons of the city's prosperity, would be shuttered as soon as dusk arrived and avoided by tourists at any cost. Recent regeneration schemes are starting to take effect, however, as projects such as the new multi-million-dollar Performing Arts Center breathe new life into this once-tacky and beleaguered neighbourhood. It is a shining example of how to transform a district from seedy to sensational.

The Downtown core revolves around its main strip, West Flagler Street. Most of the shops on this avenue cater to Miami's large Latino population, but there is also a branch of the major American department store Macy's. Also on this street is the recently restored Gusman Center for the Performing Arts, a theatre built in the 1920s with a Mediterranean exterior.

Other highlights include the Historical Museum of Southern Florida, which traces the history of the region from the first native tribes to recent waves of Cuban immigration.

To see regeneration in action, go to the stretch of Biscayne Boulevard between 13th and 14th streets. Here is where you will find the César Pelli-designed Performing Arts Center, home to some of the city's premier performing arts groups, including the Miami City Ballet and Florida

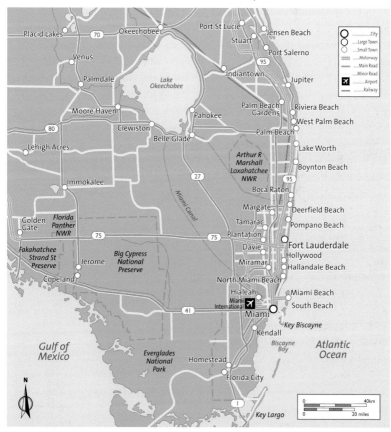

Philharmonic. A full-scale 'entertainment district' is planned to sprout up around the building, so keep your eyes open for new restaurant and boutique developments in the near future.

Bacardi Museum

After the Cuban Revolution, the Bacardí family upped and moved all of its holdings to Bermuda, the Bahamas and Miami. This museum takes a look at the famous rum-soaked family from its early days in Cuba in 1862 to the present day.

2100 Biscayne Boulevard at NE 21st Street. Tel: (305) 573 8511.
Open: Mon–Fri 9am–3.30pm.
Free admission. Bus: 3, 16, 36, 62, 95.

Historic Gesù Church

The oldest church in Miami is this 1920s structure featuring fine stained glass and exteriors inspired by Venetian architecture and design.

118 NE 2nd Street at NE 1st Avenue. Tel: (305) 379 1424. www.gesuchurch. org. English services: Sun 8.30am & 11.30am. Metromover: 1st Street.

Historical Museum of Southern Florida

Florida's history is relatively short, but this museum does a good job of bringing it to life through the use of photography, multimedia, reconstructions and informative displays.

101 W Flagler Street at NW 1st Avenue. Tel: (305) 375 1492.

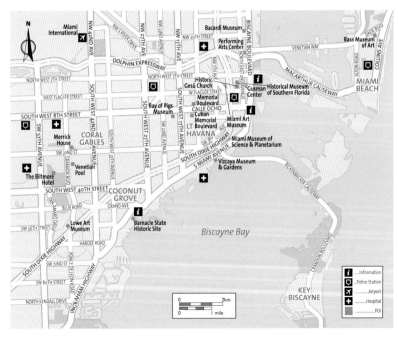

The high-rises of Downtown Miami

*www.hmsf.org. Open: Mon–Sat
10am–5pm, Sun noon–5pm,
3rd Thur of each month 10am–9pm.
Admission charge. Metromover:
Government Center.*

Miami Art Museum
This new addition to the city art scene
features up-and-coming and
established modern artists and visiting
exhibitions. A focus on making the
museum family-friendly makes it a
great place to bring the kids.
*101 W Flagler Street at NW 1st Avenue.
Tel: (305) 375 3000.
www.miamiartmuseum.org.
Open: Tue–Fri 10am–5pm, Sat & Sun
noon–5pm, 3rd Thur of each month
10am–9pm. Admission charge.
Metromover: Government Center.*

Coconut Grove
The pretty community of Coconut
Grove has had a reputation as the home
of choice for bohemians and creative
types ever since it was founded and

settled in the late 19th century by
pioneers, sea traders and fishermen
from the nearby Bahamas. The creation
of a hotel in 1882 by a New England
family drew intellectuals and writers
from the colder climes up north,
eventually resulting in the evolution of
a town known for its tolerant attitudes.

During the 1960s the district became
well known as Florida's hippie
community – a Southern Haight-
Ashbury or Greenwich Village.
Unfortunately, the hippies of the 1960s
became the yuppies of the 1980s and
pushed most artists out in order to
take advantage of the booming real-
estate market.

Today, Coconut Grove is a mix of the
typically suburban combined with
elements of its countercultural early
days. Affluent white-collar workers mix
with the remains of the artist
community, forming an independently
minded district that is both easy on the
eye and pleasant to visit. Shopping
centres rule the roost here, although

each new mega-mall development is battled by residents eager to keep Coconut Grove special.

Miami Museum of Science and Planetarium

While this museum was put together in association with the Smithsonian Institution, it is decidedly dated in both look and feel. The permanent exhibition features interactive displays that would have looked tired back in the 1980s, but it is good if you want to keep the kids occupied for an hour or two during wet weather. Visiting exhibits are more successful and tend to draw large crowds. Friday nights are the best time to visit the Planetarium, when the observatory is free to visitors.

3280 S Miami Avenue at SW 32nd Road. Tel: (305) 646 4200. www.miamisci.org. Open: 10am–6pm. Admission charge. Bus: 48. Metrorail: Vizcaya.

Vizcaya Museum and Gardens

The perfect day in Coconut Beach would not be complete without a visit to this faux-Renaissance villa built directly on Biscayne Bay. While the grounds and exteriors are more than enough to warrant stopping by, it's the interiors that intrigue most, providing a peek into what luxury lifestyles were like during the early years of the 20th century when the original owner, industrialist James Deering, built the property.

3251 S Miami Avenue at SW 32nd Road. Tel: (305) 250 9133.

Vizcaya's serene gardens

www.vizcayamuseum.org. Open: 9.30am–4.30pm. Admission charge. Bus: 48. Metrorail: Vizcaya.

Coral Gables

The community of Coral Gables is the affluent suburb of choice for industrialists, bankers and foreign politicians thanks to its cheery colours, elegant mansions and manicured vegetation. Located away from the shoreline, it is no less beautiful for it thanks to the influence of city founder George Merrick. A fan of order and precision, Merrick hired a landscape architect to transform his land into a beautiful garden city that residents could be proud of, and the results are clear to see.

An early example of a planned American community, Coral Gables combines the order of a charming residential district with the elegance of a well-preserved historic quarter complete with gates and bubbling fountains. Historic Preservation laws are some of the toughest in the country, meaning that the look and feel of Coral Gables should be ensured for plenty of years to come.

Lowe Art Museum

This eclectic museum exhibits pieces from across the millennia. Everything from Egyptian artefacts to Impressionist masterpieces is on display. Of particular note is the East Asian collection with its various treasures from Japan, China and Korea. *University of Miami, 1301 Stanford Drive at Ponce de Leon Boulevard. Tel: (305) 284 3535. www.lowemuseum. org. Open: Tue, Wed & Fri–Sat 10am– 5pm, Thur noon–7pm, Sun noon–5pm. Closed: Mon. Admission charge. Bus: 52, 56.*

Merrick House

If you like historic properties, then this house once owned by the founder of the city, George Merrick, should be of (*Cont. on p34*)

Merrick House in Coral Gables

Bike tour: Key Biscayne

Only 6³/₄ miles (11km) long – and a world away from the glitz of South Beach and raw energy of Downtown Miami – Key Biscayne is the enclave of choice for the elite of the city. The best way to see the island is by bicycle. Begin your tour with a stop at Mangrove Cycles (Tel: (305) 361 5555), located in the middle of the island just off the main bike path that runs along Crandon Boulevard. A day-long rental starts at just $15 per bike (including helmets and locks).

Depending on stops, the trip should take no more than four hours. Begin your journey by cycling north along Crandon Boulevard and then Rickenbacker Causeway for approximately 2¹/₂ miles (4km). The Miami Seaquarium will appear on your left.

1 Miami Seaquarium

As one of the first aquariums in the United States, the Miami Seaquarium boasts a long history preserving marine life and teaching visitors about conservation. Displays are broken up into zones including tropical reefs, shark tanks and rainforest areas that include examples of flora and fauna native to each location. Of specific interest are the manatee rehabilitation programmes and feeding times, so check the board when you arrive and take note of schedules.

4400 Rickenbacker Causeway. Tel: (305) 361 5705. www.miamiseaquarium.com. Open: 9.30am–6pm. Admission charge. Backtrack along Crandon Boulevard for

approximately 1¹/₄ miles (2km) to reach your next stop.

2 Crandon Park

This massive park is a highlight to any Miami visit primarily due to its pristine and popular 3-mile-long (5km) beach. Covered with mangrove swamps, the park is how Florida must have been before the creation of million-dollar homes and flashy nightclubs. Get more out of your visit by stopping off at the **Marjory Stoneman Douglas Biscayne Nature Center** (*6767 Crandon Boulevard at Crandon Park. Tel: (305) 361 6767. www.biscaynenaturecenter.org. Open: 10am–4pm. Free admission*) to learn about local ecology and plant species. *Continue along Crandon Boulevard for ³/₄ mile (1.2km).*

3 Bill Baggs Cape Florida State Recreation Area

The entire southern end of Key Biscayne makes up this state park, which boasts a great Atlantic-facing beach, boardwalk and sand dunes. Get to the park early if you want to visit the Cape Florida Lighthouse, which is your next stop on the itinerary.

Termination of Crandon Boulevard.
Tel: (850) 245 2157.
www.floridastateparks.org.
Open: 8am–sunset. Admission charge for cyclists and motorists.
Cycle south to the tip of Key Biscayne for your final stop.

4 Cape Florida Lighthouse

The Cape Florida Lighthouse was originally built in the 1820s following numerous wrecks. Destroyed during the First Seminole War, it was rebuilt in 1845. Guided tours run at 10am and 1pm every day, but you'll have to be prompt as only the first ten people to show up will be permitted to join.

From the lighthouse, enjoy the views over the island and over to Stiltsville, a collection of seven homes built on stilts off the south shore during the 1940s and 1950s by fishermen.

Bill Baggs Cape Florida State Recreation Area. Tel: (305) 361 8779.

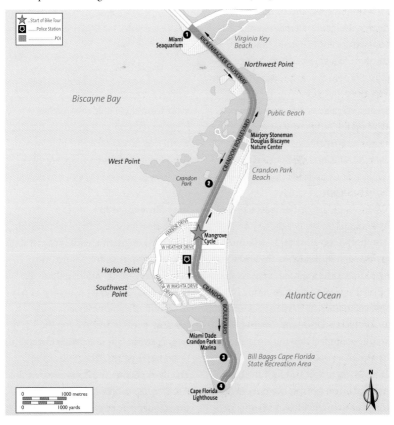

interest. Artwork, personal effects and photography provide a snapshot of life in the 1920s when Miami was only just starting to come into its own.

907 Coral Way at Toledo Street. Tel: (305) 460 5361. Open: Wed & Sun 1–4pm, tours 1pm, 2pm & 3pm. Admission charge. Bus: 24. Coral Gables Circulator.

Venetian Pool

Even if your hotel has a pool of its own, it's worth the trek to Coral Gables to feast your eyes on this lush swimming pool built from the remains of a former quarry. Sculpted waterfalls, faux-Italian architecture and jungle-like foliage combine to create a lagoon-style paradise.

2701 De Soto Boulevard at Toledo Street. Tel: (305) 460 5356. www.coralgablesvenetianpool.com. Open: daily, hours vary according to season and weather. Admission charge. Bus: 24, 72. Coral Gables Circulator.

South Beach

When visitors sit at home thinking of Miami, it is South Beach they dream of. A hodgepodge of pastel hotels and grimy bars, sleek nightclubs and slimy gigolos, South Beach has seen its share of celebrities and sin pass along its sidewalks since its heyday back in the 1920s. Ocean Drive and Collins Avenue are the strips to hang out on if sun-drenched excess is what you're after. Here is where you will find the top hotels, chicest hotspots and most hard-to-get-into nightclubs in Miami. Step

THE BILTMORE HOTEL

Miami boasts little in the way of a past, so it can come as a delightful surprise when visitors discover pieces of history scattered throughout the city streets. Built in 1925, the Biltmore was a symbol of Miami's growing popularity as a resort destination. Boasting every innovation possible at the time, it featured grand gardens, whimsical architecture inspired by Moorish design, and the finest accoutrements money could buy, including gilt chandeliers, fine bone china and gold leaf on almost every surface. Today, it is still a popular destination for fans of fine living and luxury following a multi-million-dollar renovation during the mid-1980s. Sports enthusiasts will love the swimming pool, which was once the largest in the United States. Prices start at $280 a night during the low season.

1200 Anastasia Avenue at Granada Boulevard. Tel: (305) 445 1926. www.biltmorehotel.com

away from these golden stretches, however, and pockets of South Beach's former seediness seep through, making this neighbourhood a snapshot of America in general.

Bass Museum of Art

South Beach came into its own during the 1990s, beginning with the arrival of Madonna to its sunny shores and culminating in the multi-million-dollar renovation of the Bass Museum of Art in 1999. The exhibits cover a wide range of periods and geographic regions, from Chinese prints through to Old Master works. The renovation greatly expanded the floor space of this Art Deco gem, allowing for as many as three touring exhibits to complement

the permanent collection at any one time. Check schedules to see what lectures and screenings are available on the day of your visit.
2121 Park Avenue at Collins Avenue. Tel: (305) 673 7530. www.bassmuseum.org. Open: Tue–Sat 10am–5pm, Sun 11am–5pm. Closed: Mon. Admission charge. Bus: C, G, H, L, S.

Jewish Museum of Florida

Jews have been living in Florida ever since the mid-18th century when they arrived with Spanish explorers in search of the Fountain of Youth. This excellent museum, housed in a restored Art Deco synagogue, chronicles experiences both past and present through the use of photos and artefacts. Well worth visiting for fans of local history and culture.
301 Washington Avenue at 3rd Street. Tel: (305) 672 5044. www.jewishmuseum.com. Open: Tue–Sun 10am–5pm. Closed: Mon. Admission charge. Bus: South Beach Local.

Lummus Park Beach

Probably the most popular of all the beaches that line South Beach, this golden stretch of sand gets packed with the bronzed and beautiful every weekend. Thatched huts provide shade, and the beach is dotted with Art Deco lifeguard stands and volleyball nets,

(Cont. on p38)

The lush Venetian Pool in Coral Gables

Miami and the South Atlantic Coast

Walk: Art Deco of South Beach

Geometric patterns, sleek neon, streamlined angles and whimsical tropical motifs combine to form the distinctive designs of South Beach – all available for exploration on this stroll. Before embarking on your journey, be sure to do a spot of research at the impressive Art Deco District Welcome Center, where you can join guided tours at 10.30am on Wednesdays and Saturdays or rent an audioguide for self-exploration.

This walk will take around 2 hours.

Begin your walk at the Cameo Theater located at Washington Avenue and Espanola Way.

1 Cameo Theater

The walk starts uneventfully at the Cameo Theater, a once-popular live entertainment venue. Now the Crobar nightclub, the theatre features carved palm fronds, a typical tropical motif from the period.
1445 Washington Avenue.
Continue south four blocks and look to the left for your next stop.

2 Miami Beach Post Office

Go inside this building not just to buy stamps but to admire the interior murals with a cowboy theme, created in 1939. Built in the style known as 'Deco Federal', it combined interior Deco design sensibilities with relatively plain exteriors to form an inspiring public space.
1300 Washington Avenue.

Stroll two blocks south and continue looking to your left.

3 Washington and 10th Street

A cluster of Art Deco gems exists between 10th and 11th streets in the form of the hotels Kenmore (*No 1050*), Taft (*No 1044*) and Davies (*No 1020*). More examples lie south of 10th Street

The Colony Hotel on Ocean Drive

ART DECO DISTRICT
WELCOME CENTER

1001 Ocean Drive at 10th Street.
Tel: (305) 531 3484. Open: 10am–7pm.
Bus: C, H, K, W, South Beach Local.

in the form of the Chelsea and Astor hotels. The Kenmore offers the most stunning interiors.
Go east one block on 10th Street to Collins Avenue and then turn left, going north.

4 Collins Avenue

Collins Avenue steps up the Art Deco – although more highlights are yet to come. Essex House at Collins and 10th uses portholes and smokestacks to give the building a look reminiscent of a cruise liner. Two blocks north on the left is the Marlin Hotel, a futuristic property that was built in 1938 and looks like it stepped out of the film *Metropolis*.
Keep going up Collins three blocks to reach your next stop.

5 Hoffman's Cafeteria Building

This low-rise Deco masterpiece was the inspiration for the film *The Birdcage* after serving as a drag-queen nightclub for many years. Now a deli, it features a central tower from which stretch wing-like walls, topped with red, curvy neon signs.
Go up half a block and turn right to reach Ocean Drive.

6 Ocean Drive

Ten blocks of sensational architecture stretching from 15th Street down to 5th

end the tour. Highlights include the Breakwater Hotel (*No 940*), Colony Hotel (*No 736*), Park Central (*No 630*) and Imperial (*No 650*), the last being widely considered to be the most authentic of the lot. Don't forget to make a (grim) stop at 1114 Ocean Drive where you can see the former Versace Mansion, Casa Casuarina, outside which the famous designer was murdered by serial killer Andrew Cunanan in 1997.
You can go back to your starting point by going north to the end of Ocean Drive and then west two blocks.

Walk: Art Deco of South Beach

with games played to a Latin beat. Its popularity comes at a price, however, as erosion and overuse means that there is a battle to keep the sand in place. Gays and lesbians have their own corner of the beach at 12th Street.

Ocean Drive between 5th & 15th streets.

Wolfsonian-FIU

Explore how design affects lives in this museum named after its founder, millionaire Mickey Wolfson. Most of the items on display came from Wolfson's collection, including excellent examples of stained glass and everyday objects such as postboxes formed in surprising and beautiful ways. Regular touring exhibits bring new dimensions to the already intriguing permanent collection.

1001 Washington Avenue at 10th Street. Tel: (305) 531 1001. www.wolfsonian.org. Open: Mon, Tue, Sat & Sun noon–6pm, Thur & Fri noon–9pm. Closed: Wed. Admission charge. Bus: C, H, K, W, South Beach Local.

Little Havana

Centred around the street of Calle Ocho, Little Havana was the first stop for immigrants from Cuba escaping the nation after Fidel Castro came to power in 1959. Most of the newcomers came from the higher end of society, effectively transplanting an entire social class from Havana to Miami and creating a community in the spitting image of the part of the world they had left behind. Today, the neighbourhood is populated more by Central Americans as Cubans have gained income and moved to more salubrious areas. Despite this, the community remains vibrant as Cuban-American society pumps money into local businesses and artistic centres eager to keep their vision of Cuba alive and well in a pocket of America.

Bay of Pigs Museum

The Bay of Pigs invasion is known as one of the worst foul-ups ever to occur in the history of Cuban-American relations. In 1961 a group of Cuban exiles trained by the CIA launched an operation to attack Cuba and restore American influence to the Caribbean island. The attack was soon foiled by the Cuban military, resulting in 100 deaths. The museum chronicles this chapter in Cuban politics by using various artefacts to tell the story of the brigade that never had a chance.

1821 SW 9th Street at SW 18th Avenue. Tel: (305) 649 4719. www.bayofpigsmuseum.org. Open: Mon–Sat 9am–5pm. Free admission. Bus: 8. Little Havana Circulator.

Calle Ocho (SW 8th Street)

At the heart of Little Havana lies Calle Ocho, a pulsating road filled with Latin rhythms and shops serving the needs of the Latino community. While most of the Cuban population has been replaced by recent Central American immigrants, the region still maintains a largely Cuban feel, packed with souvenir shops and Cuban restaurants that testify to the population's historical importance.

A stroll along the street gives an idea of what Havana might look like had time not stood still in the Cuban capital following the Castro takeover. Strip malls are filled with Santería *botanicas* (*see pp40–41*), cigar stores (complete with men hand-rolling their wares), Cuban memorabilia shops and mom-and-pop stores selling Cuban culinary delicacies and tropical fruits. A Walk of Fame celebrating the contributions of Cuban celebrities lies along Calle Ocho, formed by a series of pink marble stars embedded in the sidewalk. Celia Cruz's star is one of the main attractions and served as a flower-strewn shrine following her death in 2003.

Memorial Boulevard (SW 13th Avenue)

The beginning of Memorial Boulevard is marked with an eternal flame that burns in honour of the Cuban exiles who took part and were killed in the Bay of Pigs invasion. Other statues commemorate Cuban heroes including José Martí, who led the resistance against Spain when Cuba was fighting for independence. Highlights along Memorial reflect the cultures and religious beliefs of the community, including depictions of the Virgin Mary and a large tree which practitioners of the religious tradition known as Santería think of as sacred. Look at its base to see offerings of chicken bones and other ephemera.

An artistic cafeteria on Calle Ocho in Little Havana

Santería

The religion of Santería was created in Cuba by slaves from the Yoruba culture of West Africa following attempts by their plantation owners to convert them to Christianity. While the slaves were willing to accept many of the practices of Catholicism, they did not find that the religion gave them fulfilment or well-being and fused their gods to the system of saints presented by the Roman Catholic faith.

A typical religious ceremony – and it should be considered a religion despite modern-day views of voodoo as a kitsch tourist presentation – is performed to bring humans closer in touch with the Orishas, or gods, that form the basis of the natural world. Each god controls different aspects of society and is brought forth through the use of loud and rhythmic chanting and drumming, speaking in tongues and special foods.

While there is no specific place where a ceremony can be held, practitioners often rent halls in and around Little Havana and/or Hialeah for their purposes. Altars covered in sacred art, candles and offerings are set up, allowing the ceremonies to begin.

Following this, a ceremony known as the *bembé* is begun, inviting the Orisha to interact with the practitioners, causing a selected individual to begin dancing manically in order to pass on the messages being sent through him or her.

Santería followers believe that the divine can be found in many natural things, so items such as trees can be considered sacred. An example of this lies in the form of a large ceiba tree on Memorial Boulevard. Here you will find offerings left by practitioners to honour the Orishas. So, if you see random chicken bones lying on the ground, think twice before you attempt to pick them up and throw them away.

If you ask locals whether they are Santería believers, many will give you a quizzical look and deny all knowledge. Santería is considered a very private practice and some Cuban-Americans consider the religion a blasphemy or a leftover from pre-revolution days. As such, finding a ceremony to witness can be a bit of a battle. You won't find posters advertising events and there are no tours or tourist-oriented performances that allow visitors to take part or view a ritual.

In order to conduct a ceremony, numerous objects are required,

High Priest Rigoberto Zamora from Miami

including special oils, incense and candles. These items can be purchased in shops known as *botanicas*, of which there are many in the Little Havana neighbourhood. Here is where you can purchase items related to the religion and where information can be obtained about upcoming ceremonies or religious events.

Fortune-telling and the future play a large role in Santería, and you will often find spiritualists resident in Santería *botanicas*. If you want a reading, you will probably need a translator or the ability to understand Spanish, as most of the best won't be able to speak a word of English.

Botanica Negra Francisca. 1323 SW 8th Street at SW 13th Street. Tel: (305) 860 9328. Open: Mon–Sat 10am–5pm.

FORT LAUDERDALE

The community of Fort Lauderdale became notorious in the 1950s as the destination of choice for partying college students during their annual Spring Break. For a week every March, the town would be transformed into a bacchanalian paradise packed with teens and 20-somethings fuelled by beer and a lack of inhibitions.

The past couple of decades have seen a major clean-up as town laws were changed to shift the teens away and transform the resort into a destination more suitable for the moneyed set.

Dubbed the 'Venice of Florida', Fort Lauderdale is a neighbourhood filled with over 300 miles (480km) of canals on which large yachts sit catering to the rich and famous. It is also a major

Fort Lauderdale's Swimming Hall of Fame

gay resort and a year-round holiday choice for gays and lesbians from across the country.

Bonnet House Museum and Gardens

Wander the lush gardens of this historic house set on 35 acres (14 hectares) of land. While there is a guided tour available, it is much more enjoyable to wander independently. Be sure to leave time to savour the orchid collection.
900 N Birch Road. Tel: (954) 563 5393. www.bonnethouse.org. Open: Tue–Sat 10am–3pm, Sun noon–4pm (May–Nov); Tue–Sat 10am–4pm, Sun noon–4pm (Dec–Apr). Admission charge.

Fort Lauderdale Historical Museum

Located in the Riverwalk Entertainment District, this museum and collection of restored homes chronicles the history of the country and takes a look at what life was like at the turn of the 20th century. Seminole art is also displayed here in a nod to the indigenous peoples of this part of the state. For a deeper look at historic Fort Lauderdale, call ahead for a schedule of tours of the town's historic buildings.
231 SW 2nd Avenue. Tel: (954) 463 4431. www.oldfortlauderdale.org. Open: Tue–Sun 11am–5pm. Admission charge.

International Swimming Hall of Fame

Olympic memories, Hollywood epics and stars past and present are honoured in this museum with a

The 'Venice of Florida', Fort Lauderdale

collection of items from the great moments in the sport. Johnny Weissmuller, Mark Spitz and Esther Williams are all given their dues, but you may want to give it a miss unless you're a huge fan.

1 Hall of Fame Drive. Tel: (954) 462 6536. www.ishof.org. Open: Mon–Fri 9am–7pm, Sat & Sun 9am–5pm. Admission charge.

Museum of Art

Incredible modern art museum boasting a collection of works from some of the 20th century's finest artists including Henry Moore, Salvador Dalí and Andy Warhol. Also important is the growing collection of art devoted to the Southern Hemisphere.

1 E Las Olas Boulevard. Tel: (954) 525 5500. www.moafl.org. Open: Fri–Wed 11am–5pm, Thur 11am–9pm. Admission charge.

Museum of Discovery and Science

Explore the efforts Florida is making towards environmental conservation, natural sciences, the Everglades and more in this great museum that uncovers how science relates specifically to the state of Florida. Interactive displays will fascinate adults and children alike.

401 SW 2nd Street. Tel: (954) 467 6637. www.mods.org. Open: Mon–Sat 10am–5pm, Sun noon–6pm. Admission charge.

Gay and lesbian Florida

Despite the fact that Florida has some of the least progressive laws for gays and lesbians in the country, it is a favoured destination for the global homosexual population and has been so ever since artists and bohemians were lured to Key West back in the 1940s and 1950s.

Today, south Florida has one of the highest concentrations of gays and lesbians in the United States. Communities such as Fort Lauderdale, South Beach and Key West all boast significant and open gay and lesbian representation in local politics, often

Fantasyfest in Key West

influencing the rest of the nation, as alleged lesbian Janet Reno did when she became America's first female Attorney-General under President Bill Clinton. Despite this, cracks often appear just under the surface as the largely right-wing and conservative Hispanic population battles with gay activists to restrict rights relating to marriage and child-rearing.

Gay Florida really became noticeable in the late 1980s and early 1990s as HIV/AIDS became a worldwide issue and 'gay chic' was pictured in publications as prominent as *Vanity Fair* in their famous shaving photo featuring k d lang and Cindy Crawford. Madonna moved in and gay America followed, drawn by cheap, unrestored Art Deco properties in Miami, tropical lifestyles in Key West and canal-side living in Fort Lauderdale – a welcome relief following years of neglect when Key West was known as the destination of choice for AIDS-sufferers and ageing queens.

AIDS is still a worrying problem for Florida as the state has one of the highest percentages of patients in the country. It's a combination fuelled by drug use and a large immigrant population unschooled in safe sex practices.

A gay trolley tour in Key West

During the year, there are a number of events that bring in the pumped and pec'd, including Miami's annual AIDS benefit, the White Party and Fantasyfest in Key West.

The White Party, held over the course of a week every November, is America's oldest and largest AIDS benefit, having been held for over 20 years. Women's parties, renowned DJs and special events are held over the course of the seven-day affair, culminating in a big bash at the end of the week. Information can be found at *www.whiteparty.org*

Fantasyfest is less focused on the body beautiful and more on the art of having a great time. Drag shows and pet parades put the focus firmly on the kitsch and the queer. For two weeks every October, where the White Party caters to the high school star athlete, Fantasyfest is more geared towards the Drama Club type who likes sequins and sensation over pumping dance beats and shirtless hunks. Click on *www.fantasyfest.net* for more details.

If planning a holiday, consider staying at one of Florida's numerous gay- or lesbian-only establishments. Fort Lauderdale and Key West offer plenty of options, with the former serving as the headquarters of the IGLTA (International Gay and Lesbian Travel Association). For accommodation suggestions, go to *www.iglta.org*. Miami has fewer gay-specific properties, but the Art Deco masterpieces eagerly cater to gay clientele and you won't feel out of place if asking for a double bed for you and your partner.

BOCA RATON

It may not be as luxurious as Palm Beach further to the north, but Boca Raton still boasts some pretty fancy residents. Where Palm Beach caters to old money and blue bloods, Boca Raton is strictly for the brash and the new. Gated communities rule the roost as residents lock themselves in to keep their Gucci emblazoned bags, Chanel suits and flashy Ferraris well hidden from the prying eyes of those less fortunate.

The town was a dot on the map until the 1920s when architect Addison Mizner shone the global spotlight on the region after completing a 100-room hotel, the most expensive in the world upon its completion. Today, it holds the Boca Raton Resort and Club, allowing you the chance to live the life of luxury (if only for a short while).

Boca Raton Museum of Art

Everything from pre-Columbian artefacts to modern art masterpieces is housed at this eclectic museum. Contemporary works by Picasso and Matisse are displayed next to African and Asian wonders in a building situated in the heart of Boca's most popular green space, Mizner Park. *501 Plaza Real. Tel: (561) 392 2500. www.bocamuseum.org. Open: Tue, Thur & Fri 10am–4pm, Wed 10am–9pm, Sat & Sun noon–5pm. Admission charge.*

Boca Raton Resort and Club

This famous resort was what started Boca Raton's beachside boom. Built by

Boca Raton's open spaces are spotless

Addison Mizner in 1926, it has been the destination hotel of choice for the rich and discerning ever since it first opened its doors. In order to enjoy the variety of amenities, you'll have to be a guest. Better yet, snap a photo of the place on your way to one of the resort's fine dining establishments, such as Angela Hartnett's Cielo or Morimoto (sushi). *501 E Camino Real. Tel: (888) 543 1277. www.bocaresort.com*

Daggerwing Nature Center

Flock to this centre to see Florida's feathered friends in all their glory. Enjoy hiking trails through protected swampland that is home to herons, egrets and many other bird species native to the region. Night hikes are also possible and will bring you into contact with owls and other nocturnal animals.

South County Regional Park, 11200 Park Access Road. Tel: (561) 629 8760. Open: Sun & Tue–Fri 1–4.30pm, Sat 9am–4.30pm. Admission charge.

Gumbo Limbo Environmental Complex

Over 20 acres (8 hectares) of protected land provides visitors with a glimpse of one of south Florida's last untouched forest islands. Enjoy the stroll along the ¹/₂-mile (800m) boardwalk and end your journey at a 40ft-tall (12m) observation tower that features glorious views over the Atlantic coast.

1801 N Ocean Boulevard. Tel: (561) 338 1473. www.gumbolimbo.org. Open: Mon–Sat 9am–4pm, Sun noon–4pm. Donations welcome.

Morikami Museum and Japanese Gardens

Many associate Japanese-American culture and history strictly with the West Coast. However, many Japanese agricultural workers moved to Florida in order to work the orange groves and farmsteads back at the turn of the 20th century. Their story is told in this intriguing museum located north of Boca Raton in Delray Beach. Be sure to devote some time to the serene gardens that surround the main building.

4000 Morikami Beach Road, Delray Beach. Tel: (561) 495 0233. www.morikami.org. Open: Tue–Fri 10am–5pm. Admission charge.

Miami and the South Atlantic Coast

The serene Morikami Japanese Gardens

Hurricane hotspots

Summer is a season that brings fear to the heart of many a Floridian. Humid, damp and broiling hot, it can sap the energy of even the most active. Despite this, natives would be willing to live through all of it if it weren't for the fact that summer also brings hurricane season. From June to November every year, Floridians go on hurricane watch – and for good reason. Hurricane occurrences have been going up steadily over the past few years and nobody quite knows if this is a trend, an effect of global warming, or just plain bad luck.

The last major hurricane to hit Florida was Hurricane Andrew back in 1992, which left over 150,000 people homeless, but 2004 was the worst year on record when four large-scale hurricanes (Charley, Frances, Ivan and Jeanne) all affected parts of Florida with varying degrees of destruction. Of the 160 hurricanes to reach American shores between 1900 and 2000, over a third hit Florida, and if scientific predictions prove true, that figure could go up, up and away.

Essentially, a hurricane is a very bad storm with winds over 73mph (117km/h). Depressions that form over the Atlantic build in ferocity and are driven across the ocean from the African coast. With nothing to stop them, they continue to grow in strength until they hit landfall, with Florida proving to be an easy target. Recently, south Florida has been avoiding the worst of the systems as storms prefer to go over and up the Gulf of Mexico, wreaking destruction on the Panhandle. Hurricane Katrina is a good example of a hurricane that followed this route.

The general rule of thumb is that the power of a hurricane can be gauged according to the size of its eye: the smaller the eye, the more ferocious the storm. Hurricanes in the

Hurricane evacuation route sign

There's not much to stop the wind whipping in off the sea at Fort Lauderdale

Northern Hemisphere also always turn in an anticlockwise direction, meaning that once the storm hits land, areas to the north and east will be most severely affected.

Each season, the first storm of the year is given a name that starts with the first letter of the alphabet. Each subsequent storm is then given a name in alphabetical order. This helps climatologists track storm movements even during periods when there are multiple hurricanes to follow.

Hurricanes are also evaluated in terms of power. Category one hurricanes are the weakest of the bunch, while category five storms have the potential to cause terrible loss of life and mass destruction.

Due to the fact that hurricanes hit Florida so frequently, the city of Miami is the headquarters of the National Hurricane Center, the body responsible for the tracking of regional hurricanes and issuance of storm warnings. Tours of the centre can be arranged during the hurricane off-season between mid-January and mid-May. Even those who have no interest in climatology will find the 40-minute tours interesting as guides chronicle how the centre functions and records the after-effects of previous storms.

National Hurricane Center. 11691 SW 17th Street, Miami. Tel: (305) 229 4404. www.nhc.noaa.gov.
Open: tours by arrangement during mid-Jan–mid-May.

PALM BEACH AND WEST PALM BEACH

Tradition has it that the wealthy live on Palm Beach Island while their hired help reside in West Palm Beach. This isn't necessarily true, but the difference between the two communities is certainly noticeable. Palm Beach has long been the sunspot of choice for America's millionaires, with Rockefellers, Kennedys and Trumps calling the town their home away from home for generations. By far the most opulent residence is Donald Trump's Mar-A-Lago, an exclusive country club with a membership fee of $100,000 annually. West Palm Beach, while more workaday, is the place to go for more accessible nightlife, shopping and sightseeing options.

Abstract piece at the Norton Museum of Art

Henry Morrison Flagler Museum

Many consider this museum America's version of the Taj Mahal. An Edwardian masterpiece mansion, the Flagler Museum was originally built as a family home by the Standard Oil millionaire Henry Flagler and given as a gift of love to his third wife. There are over 55 rooms to explore and a restored railway car that Flagler once used to cross the country.

1 Whitehall Way, Palm Beach.
Tel: (561) 655 2833. www.flagler.org.
Open: Tue–Sat 10am–5pm, Sun
noon–5pm. Admission charge.

Lion Country Safari

This cageless safari camp was the first of its kind in America. Animals are divided according to region and encouraged to wander through the 500 acres (200 hectares). Lions, rhino and buffalo are just some of the species you may encounter as you drive your car through the grounds.

2003 Lion Country Safari Road,
Loxahatchee. Tel: (561) 793 1084.
www.lioncountrysafari.com.
Open: 9.30am–5.30pm. Admission charge.

Norton Museum of Art

A small yet perfectly formed art gallery packed with treasures. The collection is divided geographically, with American works from Pollock and Hopper in one section, French Impressionist and post-Impressionist masterpieces in another, and a vast collection of Chinese jades, bronzes and ceramics.

Worth Avenue in Palm Beach

1451 S Olive Avenue, West Palm Beach.
Tel: (561) 832 5196. www.norton.org.
Open: Tue–Sat 10am–5pm, Sun 1–5pm.
Admission charge.

Palm Beach Zoo at Dreher Park

This small zoo focuses on quality
rather than quantity. With only 500
animals on display at any one time,
don't plan on spending a complete
day here. Highlights include a pair of
rare Malayan tigers and a
reproduction rainforest.
1301 Summit Boulevard, West Palm
Beach. Tel: (561) 547 9453.
www.palmbeachzoo.org.
Open: 9am–5pm. Admission charge.

Playmobil Fun Park

For families with really small kids
(think up to 5 years old), this place is a
life-saver. Themed play areas provide

hours of fun – and with admission
costing only $1 per person, it's
surprisingly affordable.
8031 N Military Trail, Palm Beach
Gardens. Tel: (561) 691 9880.
www.playmobil.com. Open: Mon–Sat
10am–6pm, Sun noon–5pm.
Admission charge.

Worth Avenue

The rich and pampered of the South
shop till they drop on this sun-drenched
strip lying between South Ocean
Boulevard and Cocoanut Row. Over 200
boutiques line this retail paradise with
everything from high-street labels like
Benetton to top-end shops such as
Chanel offering their wares. Due to the
high calibre of the shops, you'll need to
dress more like Pretty Woman after the
makeover to fit in.
Worth Avenue, Palm Beach.

JUPITER AND JUPITER ISLAND

Jupiter is a half hour north of Palm Beach, but a world away in terms of diversions. Nature in all its glory is why travellers come to Jupiter and its island just off the coast. Here you will find plentiful trails and reserves that are sure to entrance hikers, bikers, bird watchers and swimmers with their beauty. And if that doesn't appeal, then the pristine beaches certainly will.

Blowing Rocks Nature Preserve

Hikers flock to this preserve, drawn to its mile-long (1.6km) trail highlighting the beauty of Florida's ecology. Guided tours of the trail are available on Fridays and Sundays. Manatee spotting is a particular highlight as the aquatic mammals often swim near the coast.
S Beach Road, Jupiter.
Tel: (561) 744 6668. Open: 9am–5pm.
Admission charge.

Burt Reynolds and Friends Museum

A resident of Jupiter, Burt Reynolds was the biggest box-office draw of the late 1970s and early 1980s thanks to hits like *Cannonball Run* and *Smokey and the Bandit.* Since that time his career has been less than stellar, but you wouldn't know it if you looked at the variety of autographed items and career photos on display at this kitschy museum.
100 N US Highway 1, Jupiter.
Tel: (561) 743 9955.
http://burtreynoldsmuseum.org.
Open: Fri–Sun 10am–4pm.
Admission charge.

Jupiter Inlet Lighthouse

Hibel Museum of Art

This museum is dedicated to the paintings and background of Edna Hibel. Interesting if only to see why she is the only living female artist to warrant a museum of her own in the USA.
5353 Parkside Drive, Jupiter.
Tel: (561) 622 5560.
www.hibelmuseum.org. Open: Tue–Sat 11am–5pm, Sun 1–5pm. Free admission.

Hobe Sound National Wildlife Refuge

This wildlife park is actually two parks in one: a small strip on the mainland and a refuge on the northern tip of Jupiter Island. Popular with fans of the outdoors, the park offers bike trails, bird watching opportunities galore, over 3 miles (5km) of pristine beach and sea-turtle watching walks on

Tuesdays and Thursdays in June and July (reservations necessary).

US Highway 1, Jupiter & Jupiter Island. Tel: (772) 546 6141. www.fws.gov. Open: sunrise–sunset. Admission charge.

Jonathan Dickinson State Park

Discover the pristine beauty of Florida's natural world by planning a visit to this immense state park. Over 11,500 acres (4,650 hectares) of land make up this former US army property, the bulk of which is covered with native trees and swamp systems. Unlike other parks nearby, there is no ocean frontage so don't go expecting a frolic in the waves. Instead, embark on a guided nature walk or set up camp in the Pine Grove campgrounds.

16450 SE Federal Highway, Jupiter. Tel: (772) 546 2771. Open: 8am–sunset. Admission charge.

Jupiter Inlet Lighthouse

Built in 1860, this is one of the oldest lighthouses on the Atlantic Coast. A visit takes in a small museum of local and nautical memorabilia. Get more out of your trip by joining one of the regular tours.

Intersection of Captain Armour's Way, US Highway 1 & Beach Road, Jupiter. Tel: (561) 747 8380. www.lrhs.org. Open: Sat–Wed 10am–4pm. Admission charge.

Aerial view of Jupiter Inlet

The Florida Keys

Stretching over 150 miles (240km) from the tip of Florida's mainland lie the Florida Keys, a collection of over 400 islands surrounded by emerald-green waters and linked by one of America's most spectacular highways – US 1.

Key West, the town located at the end of the road (literally), is the most popular destination for visitors to this region, drawn by the bohemian atmosphere and anything-goes attitude. Legendary author Ernest Hemingway certainly loved this town, spending 11 years living in the Keys. Today, it's a popular stop for both a large gay community and mainstream cruises.

Any journey of the Keys begins at Key Largo, the gateway to the region. Originally called Rock Harbor, today the town boasts little to entice the casual tourist (unless you really need a tacky T-shirt to add to your collection), but there's still plenty to see and do in the area. Be sure not to miss the John Pennekamp Coral Reef State Park if you are a keen diver or have any desire to explore the reefs of the region. From here, it's a straight drive of about two and a half hours to Key West. But nothing along the Keys is straight at the best of times, so be sure to plan plenty of time for diversions.

Key Largo

Of all the Keys along the chain, Key Largo is by far the least impressive. Souvenir stores and motels that have seen better days line the highway and are all best avoided. While it would be easy to drive straight through, you

Key Largo is the largest of the Keys

would be missing a number of natural gems, however, including coral reefs and ecological wonders. The island wasn't always known as Key Largo: in fact, its renaming is a relatively recent innovation following the release of the Humphrey Bogart/Lauren Bacall film noir of the same name (*see box p58*).

Dolphin Cove

Yes, it is possible to swim with dolphins if you book ahead, but this centre is actually better known for the variety of ecology tours and kayak expeditions on offer. Opening times vary, with regular tours offered throughout the season. *MM 101.9, Key Largo. Tel: (305) 451 4060. www.dolphinscove.com. Admission charge.*

Florida Keys Wild Bird Rehabilitation Center

Located just south of Key Largo in the town of Tavernier, the Florida Keys Wild Bird Rehabilitation Center is a valuable scientific research base dedicated to rehabilitating sick and (*Cont. on p58*)

Drive: Along US 1

Running 113 miles (182km) from Miami to Key West, US 1 is one of America's most spectacular drives. Linking 45 islands in total, the highway passes through resort communities, fishing villages, state parks and refuges, and it's a world away from the pulsing plasticity that Miami can sometimes resemble. The Florida Keys have always attracted independent thinkers and bohemians, so don't be surprised if a typical drive takes you past a ramshackle building or variety of crusty characters.

Begin your journey at Key Largo and continue until you reach the end of land – about 2½ hours or two weeks away depending on how fast you decide to go. See map on p55 for route.

1 Key Largo
See p54.

2 Islamorada
Islamorada isn't one island, it's actually a group of six islands located between Mile Markers 90 and 74 along US Highway 1. Fishing is the mainstay of the region, with deep-sea fishing fans flocking for miles to charter boats from the various marinas. In addition to fishing, other sites explore the history of the region, including the **Indian Key State Historic Site**, which is actually an abandoned island that once housed an Indian tribe, the preserved forest and bird watching opportunities of the **Lignumvitae Key State Botanical Site**, and the somewhat faded aquatic displays at the **Theater of the Sea**.

Indian Key State Historic Site. MM 79.5, Islamorada. Tel: (305) 664 4815. Open: tours Thur–Mon 9am & 1pm. Admission charge.
Lignumvitae Key State Botanical Site. MM 79.5, Islamorada. Tel: (305) 664 4815. Open: tours Thur–Mon 10am & 2pm. Admission charge.
Theater of the Sea. 84721 Overseas Highway, MM 84.5.
Tel: (305) 664 2431.
www.theaterofthesea.com. Open: 9.30am–4pm. Admission charge.

3 Grassy Key
Stop in Grassy Key if only to visit the illuminating **Dolphin Research Center**. The focus is on how dolphins benefit therapy, specifically with physically and mentally challenged children. Book in advance if you want a chance to swim with the on-site dolphins.
Dolphin Research Center. MM 59, Grassy Key. Tel: (305) 289 1121. www.dolphins.org. Open: 9am–5pm. Admission charge.

4 Marathon

This community is the last major stop before Key West. The town flavour is eclectic, combining lifestyle elements from all the other islands along the highway. Bohemians and grizzled souls live side by side in harmony. A great place to settle down for a day or a decade.

5 Seven Mile Bridge

A railway once ran along the entire stretch of the Florida Keys until various storms and hurricanes knocked it out of commission. Seven Mile Bridge, located at Mile Marker 47, is the longest stretch of railway remaining. An interpretive museum chronicles the history of the train line in a visitor centre housed in a red railway car.
MM 47, Pigeon Key. Tel: (305) 289 0025. Open: hours vary.

6 Bahia Honda State Park

Fans of powder-soft beaches, underwater exploration and camping will regard Bahia Honda as a true find.
MM 37, Bahia Honda Key. Tel: (305) 872 2353. www.bahiahondapark.com. Open: 8am–sunset. Admission charge for automobiles only.

7 Key West

The end of the road (*see pp58–61*).

Drive: Along US 1

Islamorada in the Florida Keys

RENAMING AN ISLAND

Key Largo wasn't always Key Largo. In fact, for many years it was known as Rock Harbor – until residents decided to cash in on the craze that followed the release of the Hollywood blockbuster starring Lauren Bacall and Humphrey Bogart in 1948. The film, which was based on a Maxwell Caulfield play, was an instant film noir classic revolving around the story of an ex-army officer visiting the hotel owned by the family of a former friend on the eve of a massive hurricane. When a mafia kingpin played by Edward G Robinson decides to ride out the storm in the hotel, all hell breaks loose and the intrigue begins. Always ready to see where a dollar might be made, locals renamed the island in order to draw tourists, and the plan worked... for a while.

While Bogart never visited Key Largo, his presence looms large in the form of various Bogart-themed establishments and the remains of the actual boat used by Bogart and Katherine Hepburn while filming *The African Queen*. To catch a glimpse of the boat, head over to the Key Largo Holiday Inn located at mile marker 100.

injured wild birds of the region. While the centre isn't geared up for extensive visitation, it does welcome drop-ins.
MM 93.6, Tavernier. Tel: (305) 852 4486. www.fkwbc.org. Open: 8am–6.30pm.

John Pennekamp Coral Reef State Park

Taking up over 50,000 acres (20,230 hectares) of land and water, this state park is paradise for divers due to its pristine stretch of coral along the southern coast of Key Largo. The variety of aquatic life is truly phenomenal and can be enjoyed by snorkelling, diving or by joining one of the regular, two-hour glass-bottom boat rides that depart from the main marina. Equipment rentals are available if you haven't managed to pack your tanks in your carry-on luggage.
*MM 102.5, Key Largo. Tel: (305) 451 1621. www.pennekamppark.com.
Open: 8am–sunset.
Admission charge.*

Key West

Tropical, bohemian Key West is literally the end of the road. Located at the very end (or beginning, depending on how you look at it) of US Highway 1, it's known as a creative hotbed and draws party people and hippies from across the country. Despite the fact that it boasts a population of just 30,000, this literally doubles during high season as cruise ships dock in the ports and a booming gay population draws even more visitors of a pink persuasion. The heart of Old Town lies at Mallory Square from which it's just a short walk to most other parts of the island.

Audubon House and Tropical Gardens

Birdwatchers will be very familiar with the name of James John Audubon, one of the most famous ornithologists who ever lived and the creator of the epic work *Birds of America*. This museum commemorates his contributions to nature and science.
*205 Whitehead Street. Tel: (305) 294 2116. www.audubonhouse.com.
Open: 9.30am–5pm. Admission charge.*

Key West Shipwreck Historeum

Savour the maritime history of Key West by pulling up a stoop to watch scenes from nautical history as performed by local actors on board the wreck of the *Isaac Allerton*.
1 Whitehead Street. Tel: (305) 292 8890. www.shipwreckhistoreum.com. Open: 9.40am–5pm. Admission charge.

Lighthouse Museum

Enjoy stunning views of Key West from the top of this lighthouse located in the centre of town. You'll have to be fit to climb the 88 steps that take you up to the top.
938 Whitehead Street. Tel: (305) 295 6616. www.kwahs.com. Open: 9.30am–5pm. Admission charge.

Little White House

President Harry Truman chose Key West as his home after his years in the White House. A visit to the property includes admission to a small museum dedicated to the leader who brought America through the tail-end of World War II.
111 Front Street. Tel: (305) 294 9911. www.historictours.com. Open: 9am–4.30pm. Admission charge.

Mel Fisher Maritime Heritage Museum

Mel Fisher was America's greatest salvage operator, having discovered the wreck of the Spanish galleon *Nuestra Señora de Atocha* in July 1985. The discovery of $400 million worth of treasure was the culmination of a lifetime of work. The life of the great salvager is honoured here and displayed next to a variety of artefacts discovered during his various searches.
200 Greene Street. Tel: (305) 294 2633. www.melfisher.org. Open: 9.30am–5.30pm. Admission charge.

Nancy Forrester's Secret Garden

This stunning garden, which took over 25 years to build, is a veritable paradise hidden in the heart of town. The collection of plants boasts some unique specimens. Romantics can even plan weddings presided over by the owner, who is also a licensed pastor.
1 Free School Lane. Tel: (305) 294 0015. www.nfsgarden.com. Open: 10am–5pm. Admission charge.

Southernmost Point of the USA

Probably the most photographed place on Key West, this striped marker is actually a bottle recycling bin marking the southernmost point of the mainland USA. The sign points out that you're just 90 miles (144km) from Cuba, making Key West closer to Havana than to Miami Beach.
Southern end of Whitehead Street.

Audubon House is set in tropical gardens

Walk: Hemingway's haunts in Key West

No resident of Key West has ever been more famous than Ernest Hemingway, the hard-drinking, ultra-macho author who spent his days creating masterpieces like To Have and Have Not *and his nights drinking himself into oblivion. Key West celebrates Hemingway's history every year during Hemingway Days, a celebration of the writer's works and life held each July, but you don't have to wait until then to explore Hemingway's Key West.*

This 2¼-mile (3.5km) walking tour of sights associated with Ernest Hemingway takes about 3 hours including stops.

Start at the Garrison Bight Marina located at the corner of Roosevelt and Eisenhower.

1 Garrison Bight Marina

Hemingway was attracted to Key West for many reasons, not least of which was its proximity to some of the finest deep-sea fishing spots in the Caribbean. This marina is where he would depart from on his adventures and where you can charter your own deep-sea fishing challenge.

1801 N Roosevelt Boulevard. Tel: (305) 809 3981. www.garrisonbightmarina.net. Open: 7am–6pm. Facing away from the marina, turn right along Eisenhower Street until you reach Palm Avenue and then turn left. Continue along Palm until it changes its name to Eaton Street. Walk until you reach Simonton Street and turn right.

2 Casa Antigua

Now called the Pelican Poop, this historic home was the location of Hemingway's first Key West residence in 1928. It was during the seven weeks he was staying in Key West that Hemingway decided to stay – which he did for the next decade.

314 Simonton Street. Tel: (305) 296 3887. Open: 10am–6pm. Admission charge. Continue along Simonton away from Eaton to Greene Street and then take a left until you hit Duval Street.

3 Sloppy Joe's

This famous bar was Hemingway's watering hole of choice, although water was the last drink of choice for the writer. Hemingway's tradition was to spend all morning writing and all afternoon and evening setting up camp with his mates at Sloppy Joe's.

*201 Duval Street. Tel: (305) 294 5717.
www.sloppyjoes.com. Open: Mon–Sat
9am–4am, Sun noon–4am.
Continue along Greene Street two blocks,
then turn left down Front Street.*

4 Key West Museum of Art and History

Dedicated to chronicling local history,
this museum boasts works from
regional artists and has a permanent
exhibition covering Hemingway's years
of residence in town. The collection
includes letters and memorabilia.
*281 Front Street. Tel: (305) 295 6616.
www.kwahs.com. Open: Mon–Fri
10am–3pm, Sat & Sun 9am–5pm.
Admission charge.
Backtrack to Whitehead Street and then*

*turn right. Your next stop will be in
about ten blocks.*

5 Hemingway Home and Museum

Visit the building that Hemingway
called home for the bulk of his time
in Key West. Purchased by a rich
uncle of Hemingway's wife in 1931,
this was where Hemingway wrote a
number of works, including *A Farewell
to Arms*. Now famous for the 50-plus
cats that are descendants of
Hemingway's first pet, it continued to
house his wife Pauline for over a
decade after their divorce until her
death in 1951.
*907 Whitehead Street. Tel: (305) 294 1575.
www.hemingwayhome.com.
Open: 9am–5pm. Admission charge.*

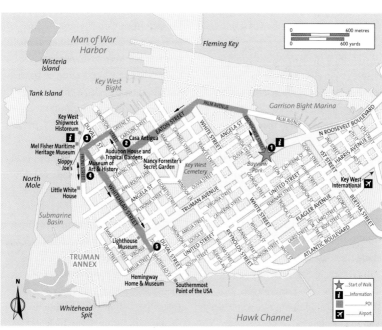

Tampa and the Gulf Coast resorts

First-time visitors to Florida tend to ignore Tampa and the Gulf Coast resorts – the less marketed and more sedate cousins to other locales in the state. To make this choice is to lose out on enjoying some of the most pristine beaches in the United States, and one of the nation's most diverse art scenes.

While Busch Gardens with its extensive collection of African wildlife and heart-pounding roller coasters is the traditional introduction to this sliver of Florida, travellers should treat a day here as merely the gateway to an incredible array of holiday options including canoeing with wild manatees in the Crystal River, learning about circus history in Sarasota or collecting shells on sleepy Sanibel Island. Begin your journey in Tampa, making sure to experience the Latin-infused nightlife of Ybor City, a once industrial part of town that is now home to some of the city's hottest restaurants and clubs. Cross the bay for a stop in St Petersburg, home to the world-renowned Salvador Dalí Museum. From here, you can go north to the family-friendly beaches of Clearwater and the wildlife of the Crystal River or south along the coast to Florida's hidden jewels – the resorts of Sarasota, Sanibel, Captiva, Fort Myers and Naples. Whether it's a booming arts scene, sleepy solitude, casual chic or sleek sophistication you're after, the Gulf Coast has it in abundance.

Tampa

This city on Florida's Gulf Coast is a sprawling metropolis that made its name as a shipping centre, primarily for tobacco from Cuba before the US embargo began in 1959. Since then, tourism has become Tampa's major draw as the city's collection of barrier islands, theme parks, never-ending sun and world-class cultural diversions have made it one of America's premier resort destinations.

Economically, Tampa is growing at a rapid rate as financial industries, high-tech firms and shipping have transformed the region into one of Florida's success stories.

Adventure Island

Cool off in the roaring waters of the various slides, waterfalls and splash pools that call this water theme park home. Over 25 acres

(10 hectares) of fun and frivolity await, offering attractions suitable for everyone from 5 to 85. Land-based diversions such as arcades and volleyball courts offer respite from the drenchings.

10001 Malcolm McKinley Drive.
Tel: (813) 987 5600.
www.worldsofdiscovery.com.
Open: 10am–5pm (mid-Mar–first
Mon in Sept); Fri–Sun 10am–5pm
(Sept–Oct).
Admission charge.

Big Cat Rescue

Get close to the big cats by visiting this sanctuary where it is possible to feed and photograph lions and tigers. True adventurers can even choose to stay on-site in one of the cabins.

12802 Easy Street. Tel: (813) 920 4130.
www.bigcatrescue.org. Open: Mon–Fri
9am–3pm. Admission charge.

Channelside

Clubs, bars, an IMAX theatre and shops all feature at this mega-entertainment

complex, and thousands visit the complex every day for its numerous diversions. The fact that the Port of Tampa is located right next door means that hordes of cruise-ship vacationers also descend on the building. Try to time your visit to avoid the swarms of holidaymakers.

Channelside Drive. Tel: (813) 223 4250. Open: 11am–7pm.

Contemporary Art Museum

The University of South Florida offers this small art gallery as an exhibition space for students both past and present. The exhibits are often interesting and worth a side trip if you are a fan of contemporary or regional work.

4202 E Fowler Avenue. Tel: (813) 974 2849. www.usfcam.usf.edu. Open: Mon–Fri 10am–5pm, Sat 1–4pm. Free admission.

Davis Island

This 'real people' neighbourhood is a great place to sit and watch the world go by. Sidewalk restaurants line the streets, allowing you to sit down and enjoy good food and great atmosphere.

Florida Aquarium

Probably the best aquarium in Florida, this amazing facility dedicated to aquatic life showcases the over 5,000 water-based plants and animals native to Florida's waters. Explore coral reefs, wander through mangrove forests, learn about shore maintenance and

Tampa's skyline

watch stingrays, sharks and moray eels as they glide through the massive tanks. Take your visit even further by booking yourself onto a 90-minute eco-tour on the aquarium's 64ft (19.5m) catamaran from which you can swim with sharks.

701 Channelside Drive. Tel: (813) 273 4000. www.flaquarium.org. Open: 9.30am–5pm. Admission charge.

Henry B Plant Museum

Formerly a ritzy hotel, this building now houses a museum devoted to art and interiors from Europe and Asia. There are also interesting permanent exhibitions that look at local history and the impact of early tourism on the region.

401 W Kennedy Boulevard. Tel: (813) 254 1891. www.plantmuseum.com. Open: Tue–Sat 10am–4pm, Sun noon–4pm. Suggested donation.

Lowry Park Zoo

While zoos are zoos the world over, this 24-acre (10-hectare) collection of animals boasts a variety of rare specimens that make it worth the trip. In addition to playful manatees there are Komodo dragons from Indonesia, red pandas and Persian leopards. Animals live in large enclosures that try to avoid the use of cages and bars when possible and are designed to resemble natural habitats. Even the aviary allows for the birds to fly freely. Small children especially love the petting zoo.

1101 W Sligh Avenue. Tel: (813) 935 8552. www.lowryparkzoo.com.
Open: 9.30am–5pm. Admission charge.

MOSI
(Museum of Science and Industry)

This interactive science museum is the largest of its kind in the southeastern United States with over 450 exhibits designed to keep kids happy and interested while they learn. Everything from the ferocity of hurricanes to the wonders of the human body is explored through interactive exhibits. The Gulf Coast Hurricane simulator allows you to experience the power of hurricane-speed winds.

4801 E Fowler Avenue. Tel: (813) 987 6100. www.mosi.org. Open: 9am–5pm. Admission charge.

Old Hyde Park

Residential neighbourhoods don't come more atmospheric than this. Old Hyde Park is widely considered to be the address of choice for Tampa's moneyed residents due to its preserved Victorian architecture, gas lanterns and brick-lined streets. Here is where the best dining and shopping options can be found. Be sure to make a side trip to Bayshore Boulevard to enjoy a stroll or bike ride along the boardwalk. Sunsets are especially glorious.

Old Hyde Park. www.oldhydeparkfl.org

Tampa Museum of Art

The constantly changing exhibits of this museum mean that every visit is different. Everything from prehistoric artefacts through to contemporary Floridian works are put on display. Check listings online before making a decision as to whether what's on will be of interest.

600 N Ashley Drive. Tel: (813) 274 8130. www.tampamuseum.org. Open: Tue–Wed & Fri–Sat 10am–5pm, Thur 10am–8pm, Sun 11am–5pm. Admission charge.

The Henry B Plant Museum

Tampa and the Gulf Coast resorts

Walk: Busch Gardens in a day

Busch Gardens is more than an amusement park or a zoo: it's a destination in its own right, drawing millions of visitors every year. For travellers in the mood for a bit of adventure, Busch Gardens is the perfect tonic. The overall theme is African in flavour, using natural environments to make the animals feel at home. You, however, might feel a bit wild after riding the park's latest roller coaster SheiKra, which takes riders up 200ft (61m) and throws them back down at a speed of 70mph (113km/h).

Begin your trip at Morocco just left of the main gate and continue around in a clockwise fashion until you return to the start. Allow at least 4–5 hours depending on queue length.

Morocco

Step inside a faux-Marrakech bazaar and enjoy craft demos, snake charmers and… an ice show?! If you need a bite to eat, the Crown Colony restaurant is the largest in the park and usually has the fastest-moving queues.

Egypt

Replica treasures from King Tut's tomb and a crazy camel-ride simulator await intrepid explorers in this zone. Those with strong stomachs can ride Montu, a roller coaster with seven loops.

Edge of Africa

Here is where you will find the big animals, including lions, rhino and giraffes. Get more out of your stay by joining a zoologist-led tour.

Nairobi

Enter the rainforest habitat of gorillas and chimpanzees at the Myombe reserve. Also here is an animal nursery, petting zoo, and a cave filled with nocturnal creatures including bats and reptiles.

The Congo

Thrill rides are the core of this zone, specifically the Kumba and Python roller coasters. If you need to cool down, join the queue for the Congo River Rapids ride, which takes riders down a swift river.

Stanleyville

Stanleyville has shops, a theatre and a collection of orang-utans – plus a couple of water rides including a flume.

Land of the Dragons

The zone for tiny tots: rides and attractions include an oversized treehouse and an echo cave.

Bird Gardens

Enter the free-flight aviary to feel the various birds fly around you. This is the original core of the park and a great place to see pink flamingos and cuddly koalas.

Hospitality House

Unlike Disney, Busch Gardens offers alcohol on-site as it's owned by the venerable Anheuser-Busch brewery, makers of Budweiser. Sample some of their more famous brews in this hospitality hut. Drinkers must be 21 or older.

Timbuktu

The final zone is this thrill-ride-focused area boasting even more roller coasters and adrenalin rides. Try to eat **after** coming to this zone.

If you want to get more out of your stay, consider registering for the 'zookeeper for a day' programme for an extra charge to shadow a keeper around the park as they carry out their daily work.
3000 E Busch Boulevard.
Tel: (888) 800 5447.
www.buschgardens.com.
Open: 10am–6pm. Admission charge.

KaTonga musical performance in 'Timbuktu'

Walk: Ybor City

Ybor City made its name as the centre for cigar making back in the days when importing Cuban tobacco was still legal. After the Cuban embargo was put in force in 1959, the district went into serious decline only to be revived over the past decade as restoration of the various warehouses transformed the area into Tampa's buzzing centre for nightlife.

This 1½-mile (2.5km) walk will take around 2 hours.

Begin your explorations at the corner of E 7th Avenue and N 21st Street.

1 Columbia restaurant

Always the heart of Ybor, 7th Avenue is the main drag of the district, and the Columbia restaurant is the oldest such establishment in all of Tampa. With 1,200 seats in 12 rooms, the Columbia is also one of the largest eateries in the world, with an exterior worth admiring if only for its Spanish excess.

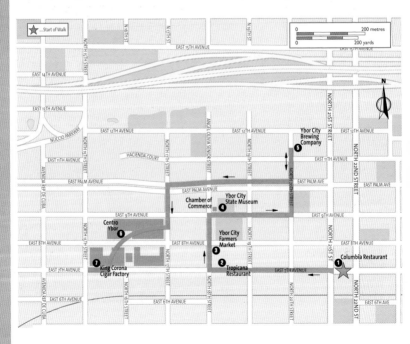

2117 E 7th Avenue. (See p179.)
Continue west towards 18th Street.

2 Tropicana restaurant

A new addition to the dining scene, the
Tropicana is now popular with local
politicos. For something a little more
blue-collar, go instead to the Silver Ring
Sandwich Shop across the street for a
genuine Cuban sandwich.
1822 E 7th Avenue.
Turn right on N 18th Street.

3 Ybor City Farmers Market

Pick up fresh fruit and veggies or local
arts and crafts at this Saturday market
held in Centennial Park. If you're visiting
on an off-day, go instead just to admire
the statue honouring the immigrant
population that made Ybor City great.
E 8th Avenue at N 18th Street.
Continue north on N 18th Street and
then turn right at E 9th Avenue.

4 Ybor City State Museum

Located in a former bakery, this
museum chronicles the history of cigar
making in Ybor City, including
collections of cigar memorabilia, labels,
advertising and photographs. Walking
tours led by local historians are
available every Saturday morning and
include a stop at a worker's cottage
called **La Casita** next to the museum.
1818 E 9th Avenue. Tel: (813) 247 1434.
www.ybormuseum.org.
Open: 9am–5pm. Admission charge.
Continue along E 9th Avenue and then
turn left at N 20th Street.

5 Ybor City Brewing Company

Once a cigar factory, now a brewery.
See what you'll be drinking later in the
district by visiting this beer-making
factory, which produces brands such as
Ybor Gold. None of the beers produced
on-site is made using any preservatives.
2205 N 20th Street.
Go back to E Palm Avenue, turn right,
then walk to N 17th Street, and turn left.

6 Centro Ybor

Yes, it's a mall, but it's also considered
the heart of the district. Depending on
your mood, go to catch a movie or a
comedy act, or dine in one of the
many restaurants.
1600 E 8th Avenue. Tel: (813) 242 4660.
www.centroybor.com. Open: 9am–11pm.
Cross through the shopping centre and
emerge from the E 7th Avenue exit, then
turn right to reach your final stop.

7 King Corona Cigar Factory

The largest cigar store in all of Ybor
City. Unfortunately, none of the old
Cubans is sold. There's even a barber
shop where you can get your hair cut
while you puff.
1523 E 7th Avenue. Tel: (888) 248 3812.
www.kingcoronacigars.com. Open:
10am–11pm.

Ybor City is quieter during the day

Ybor City State Museum

Find out more about the lives of the Cuban cigar workers who originally lived in Ybor City during its heyday. See cigar-rolling demos and visit a reconstructed home to explore the living conditions of yesteryear. For more about Ybor City, see the walk (*pp68–9*).

1818 E 9th Avenue. Tel: (813) 247 1434. www.ybormuseum.org. Open: 9am–5pm. Admission charge.

St Petersburg

Unlike its neighbour Tampa, St Petersburg was never intended as a place for industry and activity. Here is where the Northerners came to tan and ride through the cold months. Today, Floridians have taken over this extremely liveable place, transforming it from a sleepy resort to an arts-drenched, sun-soaked centre that appeals to both teens and retirees.

Florida Holocaust Museum

Founded by a local businessman who escaped Nazi Germany in 1939, this museum is now the fourth largest in the United States dedicated to chronicling the Holocaust. The displays, including a train car once used to transport victims to Auschwitz, are thought-provoking, and the collection has the goal of promoting cultural understanding and tolerance.

55 5th Street S. Tel: (727) 820 0100. www.flholocaustmuseum.org. Open: Mon–Fri 10am–5pm, Sat & Sun noon–5pm. Admission charge.

St Petersburg's Salvador Dalí Museum houses the world's largest collection of the Spanish surrealist's work

Florida International Museum

An affiliate museum of the Smithsonian, this former department store now houses some of the world's best travelling exhibitions. A permanent display about the Cuban Missile Crisis is also of interest to those with a yen to learn more about Florida's recent history.

244 2nd Avenue N. Tel: (727) 341 7900.
www.floridamuseum.org.
Open: Mon–Sat 9am–6pm, Sun noon–6pm. Admission charge.

Great Explorations

When the rain comes (and it rarely does), bring the kids to this hands-on science museum that teaches as it entertains. Located next to the Sunken Gardens, it makes for a full day of fun.

1925 4th Avenue N. Tel: (727) 821 8992.
www.greatexplorations.org.
Open: Mon–Sat 10am–8pm, Sun 11am–5pm. Admission charge.

Museum of Fine Arts

This elegant museum, which resembles a Mediterranean villa, boasts a cross-section of art from Europe, America and Asia, including a number of French Impressionist masterpieces. Other highlights include a collection of Steuben glass, and rooms dedicated to the decorative arts.

255 Beach Drive NE. Tel: (727) 821 6443.
www.fine-arts.org. Open: Tue–Sat 10am–5pm, Sun 1–5pm.
Admission charge.

St Petersburg Pier

Pier

Formerly a railway pier, this modern-day shopping centre was built in 1889 and is today a carnival-like collection of shops, decks, restaurants and more. Enjoy a stroll along the observation level, putt a game of mini-golf or join one of the cruise boats that take pleasure trips during the winter season.

800 2nd Avenue NE. Tel: (727) 821 6443.
www.stpete-pier.com. Open: Mon–Thur 10am–9pm, Fri & Sat 10am–10pm, Sun 11am–7pm.

Salvador Dalí Museum

This vast museum holds more works by the Spanish artist than any other museum. Guided tours are a must to understand the concepts behind each work and the contribution Dalí made to the art world as a whole. A new museum is currently under construction within the Progress Energy Center for the Arts, and the collection will move there in winter 2011.

1000 3rd Street S. Tel: (727) 823 3767.
www.salvadordalimuseum.org. Open: Mon–Wed, Fri & Sat 9.30am–5.30pm, Thur 9.30am–8pm, Sun noon–5.30pm. Admission charge.

Tampa and the Gulf Coast resorts

Sunken Gardens

These beautiful gardens, covering 7 acres (3 hectares), are home to a delightful collection of plants, flowers and trees through which you can wander to your heart's content. Be sure to also stop by the butterfly house, rainforest display and insectorium.
1825 4th Street N. Tel: (727) 551 3100. www.stpete.org/sunken. Open: Mon–Sat 10am–4.30pm, Sun noon–4.30pm. Admission charge.

Clearwater

Clearwater is Tampa's and St Petersburg's beachside playground of choice, with powder-soft beaches, protected mangrove channels, watersports and boating options galore. The beaches along this coast are regularly ranked among some of the nation's finest, although many are lined by massive resort complexes. Even if you are staying in one of them, do yourself a favour by budgeting time to visit one of the great local parks or public beaches that often boast the best views and quietest seaside corners.

Clearwater Marine Aquarium

This aquarium focuses less on displaying fish and more on educating the public about the preservation and conservation of the world's waterways. Highly recommended is the 'dolphin trainer for a day' package that teaches you the skills needed to work with dolphins and gives you a fascinating two-hour water safari that comes complete with the guidance

Cannon at Fort De Soto Park

of one of the on-site marine biologists.
249 Windward Passage. Tel: (727) 441 1790. www.cmaquarium.org. Open: Mon–Fri 9am–5pm, Sat 9am–4pm, Sun 11am–4pm. Admission charge.

Fort De Soto Park

Located on Mullet Key, this 900-acre (365-hectare) park is a dedicated animal, plant and bird sanctuary famous for its fort dating from the Spanish-American War and for its incredible powder beaches. Active types will adore the range of options available, from hiking to biking, fishing, jogging and more. Join one of the regular tours that lead nature lovers around the area, or rent a kayak and explore the mangroves.
3500 Pinellas Byway, Tierra Verde. Tel: (727) 582 2267. www.fortdesoto.com. Open: 8am–dusk. Free admission.

John's Pass Village and Boardwalk

Some find this 'Old Florida' fishing village over-commercialised. Others feel it's a charming village with appeal. Originally a bustling fishing community during the 19th century, the homes have since been transformed into a collection of fine-dining establishments, artist studios and unique boutiques surrounding the boardwalk and marina.

12901 Gulf Boulevard, Madeira Beach.
Tel: (727) 394 0756.
www.johnspass.com.
Open: 9am–6pm.

Pier 60

Head to this lively pier at sunset to enjoy the live carnival of buskers, musicians and artists that converge on the area every evening. By day, the swimming at the nearby beach is popular among those who want a happening scene and a wide range of activities. Fishing from the pier is also a popular pastime. By night, it's a great place to stroll and watch the golden rays sink below the horizon.

Sand Key Park and Beach

Consistently ranked as one of the top beaches in the United States, this family-friendly strip of sand boasts fine shelling and dolphin-spotting opportunities. At ½ mile (800m) in length and with a wide shoreline, it offers the most space to spread your towel, making it the best bet on crowded weekends.

1060 Gulf Road. Tel: (727) 464 3347.
Open: 7am–sunset.

Suncoast Seabird Sanctuary

This sanctuary dedicated to rehabilitating sick birds and releasing them back into the wild is the nation's largest, with over 500 'patients' on-site at any one time.

18328 Gulf Boulevard, Indian Shores.
Tel: (727) 391 6211.
www.seabirdsanctuary.com.
Open: 9am–sunset. Free admission.

Clearwater is a popular base for sailing holidays

The sacred manatee

Otherwise known as 'sea cows', manatees are gentle creatures that have got themselves on the endangered species list due to their naturally trusting nature. Playful and lovable, they grow to as large as 12ft (3.5m) in length, and weigh up to 3,500lb (1,600kg).

Manatees have one major enemy: man. Speedboats cut through them like knives through paper ribbons in the shallow coastal waters, while industrial pollution affects breeding and migration patterns as it artificially increases water temperatures.

Manatees can sometimes be hard to spot beneath the surface

Many believe that the mermaid myth was begun by sailors who saw these aquatic animals, although you'd be hard-pressed to believe it if you saw one. Resembling an underwater elephant, manatees graze on sea-grasses that they collect on their dives. They can stay below the surface for as long as 20 minutes, but usually pop up for air every 3 to 5 minutes.

Manatee numbers have been steadily dropping ever since 1973, despite numerous attempts to bolster the population. While their natural life span is about 60 years, few reach this age and low birth rates have been doing little to help. Florida law prevents breeding manatees in captivity, so research centres focus on their care and rehabilitation.

One of the best places to witness a manatee in the wild is in and around the Crystal River north on Interstate 19 from Tampa. The best season for spotting them is winter, as the warmer waters in the area draw the playful animals in their droves. Whatever you do, don't go near them, as it is against the law to touch them in their natural habitat. Snorkelling trips are provided by all of the dive centres in the region and these allow you to get close (but not

You must keep your distance from wild manatees

too close) to manatees, with prices starting at about $30 for a one-hour session. You can even stay at villas directly on the waterfront in order to enjoy the option of renting a boat to begin your day wildlife spotting.

Other locations that offer great manatee encounters include Blue Spring State Park in central Florida near Orange City, and Fort Pierce, where there is a Manatee Observation Center that focuses on educating visitors about the conservation practices in operation to keep manatees alive.

One organisation doing its bit to inform the population about the plight of the manatee is **Save the Manatee** (*www.savethemanatee.org*). This serves to provide interested environmentalists and travellers with information about their conservation programmes, volunteer possibilities and an extensive list of locations where manatees can be seen. One of the best resources for finding out more about manatees is Save the Manatee's extensive FAQ and Myths lists, which dispel incorrect information about the animals and attempt to alleviate worries Florida residents might have about how conservation methods affect them. If you have children, why not access the organisation's educational materials to add a dimension to their manatee-meeting experience? If you are considering renting a speedboat or motorised boat during your holiday, tips are also available online for boaters to ensure they do no damage.

Bradenton

There's nothing bad about Bradenton, it just happens to be surrounded by lots of places with bigger names and more widespread attractions. This residential town is the quintessential American suburb in that it's a nice place to drive through but rather beige to visit. Despite that, there are a few attractions that make for enjoyable diversions on your way to some of the larger and more notable resorts on the Gulf Coast.

De Soto National Memorial

The explorer Hernando de Soto founded settlements in the Bradenton area way back in 1539 and this reconstructed visitor attraction attempts to re-create the look and feel of life for the intrepid European few who first came to this part of Florida. Diversions include a reconstructed campsite, a walkable trail through mangroves to the location of some of the original settlement sites, and a number of actors in period clothing who attempt to show what life might have been like for the Spanish in 16th-century America.
De Soto Memorial Highway.
Tel: (941) 792 0458. www.nps.gov/deso.
Open: 9am–5pm. Free admission.

Gamble Plantation

There are few plantations left in Florida and fewer still south of the Panhandle. This historic home is a major exception and a delightful one at that. Built in the 1840s, it was constructed using tabby mortar, a local building method that combined crushed oyster shells, sand, water and molasses into a kind of primitive cement. There are ten rooms and a veranda that surrounds the antebellum-style house on three sides. Most interesting is the fine collection of 19th-century furnishings that speak of a time when the South's agricultural might brought power and money to the region at the expense of slaves. A wander through the grounds is possible at all times, but trips inside the home are by organised tour only.

Re-creation of an Indian settlement, De Soto National Memorial

Blinding white sand on Bradenton beach

3708 Patten Avenue, Ellerton.
Tel: (941) 723 4536. www.
floridastateparks.org/gambleplantation.
Open: Thur–Mon 9am–4.30pm.
Admission charge for tour only.

Solomon's Castle

A true American original. In 1974 a
metal and wood sculptor by the name
of Howard Solomon decided to build a
castle in a swamp using only items
discarded by society. The result is a
wild, wacky and whimsical 12,000sq ft
(1,115sq m) of castle made from
printing plates, beer cans, oil drums
and so much more. It truly has to be
seen to be believed.
4533 Solomon Road, Ona. Tel: (863) 494
6077. www.solomonscastle.org.
Open: Tue–Sun 11am–4pm (Oct–Jun).
Admission charge.

South Florida Museum and Parker Manatee Aquarium

If you haven't spotted a manatee
already on your trip, this aquarium is a
great place to catch a glimpse of one of
these gentle creatures of the sea,
including Snooty, the oldest manatee in
captivity, born in 1948. The South
Florida Museum focuses on telling
Florida's history from the age of the
native tribes to today. The museum has
undergone a multi-million-dollar
renovation that has refreshed its
interiors and exhibitions.
201 10th Street W. Tel: (941) 746 4131.
www.southfloridamuseum.org.
Open: Mon–Sat 10am–5pm, Sun
noon–5pm (Jan–Apr & Jul); Tue–Sat
10am–5pm, Sun noon–5pm (May–Jun
& Aug–Dec).
Admission charge.

Sarasota

Some call Sarasota Florida's version of God's waiting room, packed as it is with retirees and those living out their golden years. To brand it with this label is to do it an injustice, however, for Sarasota is attractive to more mature residents simply due to its many cultural attractions. Former resident and circus king John Ringling transformed Sarasota with his many contributions, not least of which is the exquisite Ringling Museum of Art built in the Italian Gothic and Renaissance styles.

Art Center Sarasota

When dropping into the Sarasota Convention and Visitors Bureau be sure to go next door to this community art space to enjoy displays of work from local artists. The collection is surprisingly diverse and interesting. Check schedules for demonstrations, lectures and events.

707 N Tamiami Trail. Tel: (941) 365 2032. www.artsarasota.org. Open: Tue–Sat 10am–4pm, Sun noon–4pm.

G Wiz (Gulfcoast Wonder and Imagination Zone)

Explore the worlds of the health, physical and earth sciences at this hands-on museum featuring a regularly changing collection of exhibits on loan from the Exploratorium in San Francisco.

1001 Boulevard of the Arts.
Tel: (941) 906 1851. www.gwiz.org.
Open: Tue–Sat 10am–5pm, Sun noon–5pm. Admission charge.

Sculpture at Marie Selby Botanical Gardens

Marie Selby Botanical Gardens

Over 20,000 exotic plants and flowers are to be found here. Orchids constitute the bulk of the most exquisite specimens, planted in a variety of locales including greenhouses, palm groves, pavilions and ferneries. A great place for a brief break and fantastic photo opportunities.

811 S Palm Avenue. Tel: (941) 366 5731. www.selby.org. Open: 10am–5pm. Admission charge.

Mote Aquarium

This is one of Florida's better aquariums. Interactive displays allow visitors to touch stingrays, watch sharks and witness manatees frolicking in the water. A 12-minute film showcasing the feeding and care of sharks on-site begins the journey and is followed up

by a number of exhibits that chronicle the work and research going on at the centre. If you have the time, book yourself on a two-hour cruise that takes a look at local marine life.
1600 Ken Thompson Parkway.
Tel: (941) 388 4441. www.mote.org.
Open: 10am–5pm. Admission charge.

Pelican Man's Bird Sanctuary

Over 6,000 birds are rehabilitated every year at this sanctuary dedicated to nursing some of nature's more fragile creatures back to health. Most of the birds are pelicans, which usually injure themselves after getting caught up in fishing line. While most of the birds are released, many stay on permanently. The sanctuary is temporarily closed due to funding issues.
811 S Palm Avenue. Tel: (941) 366 5730.
www.selby.org. Open: 10am–5pm.
Admission charge.

Sarasota Classic Car Museum

This museum is not just a collection of antique cars, it's also dedicated to the preservation and restoration of classic automobiles including Rolls-Royces and sports cars from over the decades. Other highlights include authentic Edison gramophones, a variety of music boxes and Penny Arcade games from before the dawn of the computer chip.
5500 N Tamiami Trail. Tel: (941) 355 6228. www.sarasotacarmuseum.org.
Open: 9am–6pm. Admission charge.

Tampa and the Gulf Coast resorts

Fighting Crime in Florida by Jack Dowd, outside Art Center Sarasota

Ringling Brothers Circus

Come one, come all to the Ringling Brothers Circus. Sarasota was the winter home of the great ringmaster John Ringling, and his influence remains strong on the area's cultural scene to this day. Until recently, Sarasota also housed a famous clowning school, which has since closed as demands for clowns have lessened over the years. Despite this, the circus remains a well-loved art form in Sarasota thanks to the donations the original founder made to the place during his years of residence.

The Ringling Brothers Circus was founded in 1884 by seven brothers, with John acting as the charismatic front man. The thing that differentiated the Ringling Brothers Circus from others of its time was its respect for its audience. Games of chance such as Three Card Monte were banished from the tents in favour of spectaculars that showcased human and animal skill. Common practices such as short-changing on tickets were also stopped in order to encourage repeat visitation.

The decision by the brothers to purchase railway cars in 1889 transformed the industry as it allowed the circus to travel across the country in order to bring the show to even greater numbers, all year round. As the weather changed, the circus moved south, eventually coming to stop in Sarasota where the staff would set up camp and ride through the winter months before going on the road again.

In 1919, the circus merged with its greatest rival Barnum & Bailey to form the self-proclaimed 'Greatest Show on Earth' – which it was until tastes changed and organisations like Cirque du Soleil came into greater favour.

At the heart of Sarasota is the **Ringling Museum Complex**, a vast estate where Ringling and his wife lived in sumptuous surroundings. Highlights of the complex include the couple's collection of Old Masters, a glorious rose garden and fascinating Circus Museum.

The art museum was gifted to the state upon Ringling's death in 1936. A knowledgeable buyer, Ringling put together a first-rate collection of masterpieces including works by Rubens and Van Dyck, tapestries, and sculptures from the Greek and Roman empires. Also here is the horseshoe-shaped **Asolo Theater**, which was transported, brick-by-brick, from a castle in Asolo, Italy. The season (October to April) is performed in repertory by professionals and

The ballroom ceiling at Ca d'Zan

graduate students from Florida State University's School of Theatre in Tallahassee and the results are often outstanding. FSU's theatre programme is considered to be one of the top ten in the country, having produced actors such as Burt Reynolds and Faye Dunaway.

The Ringling home, known as **Ca d'Zan**, is a glorious mishmash of various European styles boasting an incredible view of Sarasota Bay. The ballroom is especially stunning due to the ceiling paintings done by the former set decorator of the Ziegfeld Follies. The interiors are incredibly lavish and take everything to an almost theatrical level, reflecting the manner in which Ringling made the bulk of his money.

Finally, there is the **Circus Museum**, which examines the history of the circus as a form of entertainment, including miniature versions and circus wagons.

Ringling Museum Complex.
5401 Bayshore Road. Tel: (941) 351 1660. www.ringling.org.
Open: 10am–5.30pm.
Admission charge.

Fort Myers

Neither a relaxed backwater nor a buzzing scene, Fort Myers is the resort that can't decide what it wants to be. Not much went on in this town until the arrival of Thomas Edison in 1886 following the death of his beloved first wife. After that, the place was never the same again as bright lights and rich industrialists made the area a focal point for business. After Henry Ford moved in next door to Edison, even more entrepreneurs decided to join them. Today, it's a popular place for retirees, families and everyone in between, but you can't help thinking it's a place to go on the way to somewhere else.

Inside the Edison home

Edison and Ford Winter Estates

For many visitors, the two estates owned by the Ford and Edison families are the raison d'être for any trip to Fort Myers. Edison first arrived at the Victorian property in 1886 and spent every winter of his life there until his death in 1931. The property looks exactly as it did in 1947 when the estate was willed to the town by Edison's wife. The gardens are especially peaceful and remain as manicured as they were in Edison's day.

Directly next door is Mangoes, the winter home of Henry Ford. Both properties can only be seen on a guided tour. If you have extra time, give yourself an hour to enjoy a river ride on Edison's boat *Reliance*.
2350 McGregor Boulevard. Tel: (239) 334 3614. www.edison-ford-estates.com.

Open: Mon–Sat 9am–5.30pm, Sun noon–5.30pm, boat rides Mon–Fri 9am–3pm. Admission charge.

Imaginarium

On wet days, this interactive science museum is a life-saver for families. Packed with over 60 hands-on exhibits, it's a favourite with children thanks to its fun displays about weather, pollution, fossils and the aquatic world.
2000 Cranford Avenue. Tel: (239) 321 7420. www.cityftmyers.com/ imaginarium. Open: Mon–Sat 10am– 5pm, Sun noon–5pm. Admission charge.

Koreshan State Historic Site

In 1894, religious guru Cyrus Reed Teed upped sticks from Chicago to found a settlement of followers of his

religion. They called themselves Koreshans and believed that they actually lived inside the planet and not on the surface. Wacky it may be, but the area possesses a gentle beauty that is especially favoured by kayakers, so it's worth a visit if you want to combine cults with canoeing.
US 41 at Corkscrew Road, Estero. Tel: (239) 992 0311. www.floridastateparks.org/koreshan. Open: 8am–sunset. Admission charge.

Seminole Gulf Railway

Built in 1888, this railway used to have two lines: one running between Arcadia and Naples and a second travelling the route via Bradenton and Sarasota.

Today, it is used strictly for themed murder-mystery nights including dinner.
Colonial Station, Colonial Boulevard & Metro Parkway. Tel: (239) 275 8487. www.semgulf.com. Open: departures Wed–Sat 6.30pm, Sun 5.30pm. Charge for performances.

Southwest Florida Museum of History

Exhibits include a retired Pullman railway car, Calusa and Seminole Indian artefacts, local fossils, military history (including a Spanish cannon) and a history of the founder of the town, Colonel Myers.
2031 Jackson Street. Tel: (239) 321 7430. www.swflmuseumofhistory.com. Open: Tue–Sat 10am–5pm, Sun noon–4pm. Admission charge.

Planetary Court, Koreshan State Historic Site

Sanibel Island

A visit to Sanibel Island is both the natural highlight of any trip to Florida's Gulf Coast and a bit of a trial. Renowned for its beauty and shell-collecting possibilities, it's a stunning strip of land that has been made even more desirable due to the island's ban against further development. Despite this, falling in love with Sanibel can take a bit of work as the locals are very protective of their way of life. They know they're on to a good thing and like to keep it a bit of a secret from the rest of the world, so don't expect any warm welcomes, just some warm sunshine.

Bailey-Matthews Shell Museum

It makes sense that one of the world's foremost centres for shell collecting is also home to an amazing museum dedicated to shells and the animals that live in them. Not only are there examples on display, but there are also descriptions of how the shells have influenced science, art and literature.
3075 Sanibel-Captiva Road.
Tel: (239) 395 2233.
www.shellmuseum.org.
Open: 10am–4pm. Admission charge.

CROW (Clinic for the Rehabilitation of Wildlife)

Thousands of animals are rehabilitated here each year, of which 80 per cent were originally harmed through interaction (accidental and otherwise) with humans. This centre nurses the animals back to health, releases them back into the wild and educates humans about the perils they may pose when dealing with wildlife.
3884 Sanibel-Captiva Road.
Tel: (239) 472 3644. www.crowclinic.org.

The Bailey-Matthews Shell Museum

Open: tours Mon–Fri 11am, Sun 1pm.
Admission charge.

J N 'Ding' Darling National Wildlife Refuge

Two-thirds of Sanibel Island is protected against development and this wildlife refuge makes up a large part of that. Over 6,000 acres (2,430 hectares) of land are home to alligators, turtles and a whole range of birds including rare bald eagles. Depending on how much time you have to spend, you can enjoy either the 4-mile (6.5km) Wildlife Drive or the 2-mile (3km) hiking and biking Indigo Trail. Take your visit to the next level by booking an interpretive tour or kayak trip through **Tarpon Bay Explorers** (*Tarpon Bay Road. Tel: (239) 472 8900. www.tarponbayexplorers.com*), a local adventure centre with options good enough for beginner outdoor fanatics as well as more advanced adventurers.

Sanibel-Captiva Road. Tel: (239) 472 1100. www.dingdarlingsociety.org. Open: Sat–Thur 7.30am–sunset. Admission charge.

Sanibel Lighthouse

Sanibel Historical Village and Museum

Step back in time to turn-of-the-20th-century Sanibel in this reconstructed village complete with authentic homes and shops from the early years of the 1900s. Displays include mock-up shop fronts, old photos and memorabilia from many ages. There is also a small section of artefacts from the native Calusa tribe that called Sanibel home before the arrival of Europeans.

950 Dunlop Road. Tel: (239) 472 4648. www.sanibelmuseum.org. Open: Wed–Sat 10am–4pm. Admission charge.

Sanibel Lighthouse

Although it isn't open to visitors, Sanibel Lighthouse is still a picturesque spot overlooking the gateway to San Carlos Bay. Built in 1884, it used to be permanently manned but has since gone the way of similar structures and is fully automated.

Periwinkle Way.

Walk: Strolling through Sanibel

Sanibel is made to be strolled. As a wildlife refuge, it's a relaxing locale where driving is discouraged and the simpler pleasures of a cycle ride or sunset walk bring the surroundings to life.

Begin your day at the J N 'Ding' Darling National Wildlife Refuge on Sanibel-Captiva Road. Allow 5 hours for this 7-mile (11km) walk.

1 J N 'Ding' Darling National Wildlife Refuge

Use this refuge as a base or make a full day of it by wandering through the 6,000 acres (2,430 hectares) of land inhabited by thousands of birds (*see p85*). If you're feeling adventurous, the 2-mile (3km) Indigo Trail is sure to please.

From the entrance, turn left and cross the street.

2 Sanibel-Captiva Conservation Foundation

Almost 5 miles (8km) of nature trails await at this conservation centre dedicated to the preservation of native plant varieties. Guided tours last about 90 minutes, or join the two-hour boat cruise if you want to rest your feet.

Continue east along the Sanibel-Captiva Road.

3 Bailey-Matthews Shell Museum

Sanibel is Florida's most famous place for shell collecting, with addicts coming from miles around to add to their collections. Learn more about the varieties at this museum, which has an extensive selection of examples (*see p84*). The shells on display come from across the globe and showcase some intriguing types, the likes of which you will probably have never seen before.

Continue east along the Sanibel-Captiva Road and go back across to the north side of the street.

4 Tarpon Bay Recreation

Rent a canoe or kayak to explore the waters of gentle Tarpon Bay. Many native birds live in the bay, making this the perfect spot to do a bit of bird watching. Bald eagles are a common sight.

Turn right from Sanibel-Captiva Road and then the next left to join up with Periwinkle Way. Your next stop will be on the left-hand side of the street.

5 Sanibel Historical Village and Museum

Already a sleepy island, it gets even sleepier at this restored village that takes you back in time by about a century. Authentic early 20th-century homes line the streets of the village, evoking Sanibel's heyday as a peaceful coastal resort (*see p85*).

Continue east along Periwinkle Way until you reach the end of the road – literally.

6 Lighthouse Point

Try to time your final stop at Lighthouse Point with the sunset, as the views at this time are absolutely awe-inspiring. The Gulf Waters are given a sun-dappled glow by the orange rays that can be seen from the Sanibel Lighthouse, which has marked the entrance to San Carlos Bay since 1884. While the lighthouse is now fully automated and therefore closed to the public, it's still a great place to end your day.

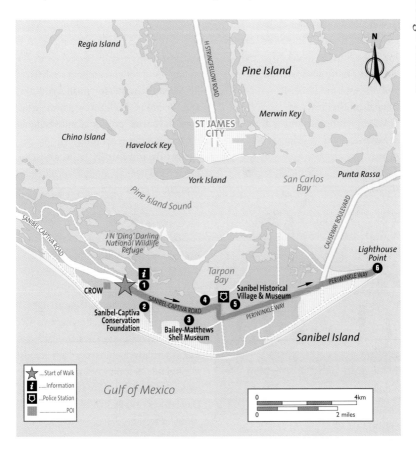

Regia Island

H STRINGFELLOW ROAD

Pine Island

Merwin Key

ST JAMES CITY

Chino Island

Havelock Key

York Island

San Carlos Bay

Punta Rassa

Pine Island Sound

SANIBEL-CAPTIVA ROAD

CAUSEWAY BOULEVARD

J N 'Ding' Darling National Wildlife Refuge

Tarpon Bay

Lighthouse Point ❻

PERIWINKLE WAY

CROW

★ ❶ 🛈

❷

Sanibel-Captiva Conservation Foundation

SANIBEL-CAPTIVA ROAD

❸ Bailey-Matthews Shell Museum

❹ 🛡 ❺

Sanibel Historical Village & Museum

PERIWINKLE WAY

Sanibel Island

Gulf of Mexico

★ ....Start of Walk
🛈 .....Information
🛡 ...Police Station
▦ ....POI

0 ——————— 4km
0 ——————— 2 miles

Captiva Island

Located north of Bowman's Beach across the Blind Pass lies Captiva Island, a small community of just a few hundred residents that is less a destination and more a day trip from Sanibel. In terms of sights, there isn't all that much on offer. This is more of a refuge away from the pressures of the world and locals are all too aware of this reputation. Go to Captiva if simple pleasures are what you desire: boat trips, beach walks, golf and sunset viewing. Not a place for children, it's the perfect place for romantic couples and those looking to de-stress and savour the natural surroundings.

Chapel-by-the-Sea

Tiny yet picturesque, this intimate, non-denominational church is a

Chapel-by-the-Sea is popular for weddings

THE SHELL GAME

The islands of Sanibel and Captiva offer some of the most diverse varieties of shells on the planet, with over 160 on display at any one time on the beaches and shores. Shell collecting is a popular pastime and it's possible to come home with a bucket-load of varieties following even the briefest of strolls along the sand. Locals claim that the best shell collecting can be found at Blind Pass in the northwest of Sanibel. Go at low tide and join the crowds as they hunt out conch shells and slippers. Whatever you do, make sure there aren't any residents still living in the shells you select, as taking a living shell is grounds for a huge fine. This goes for sea urchins and sand dollars too: when in doubt, leave it in the water.

testament to yesteryear. Built in 1904, it's a popular venue for small weddings and functions. The nearby cemetery has been the burial spot for island residents throughout the generations.

11580 Chapin Lane. Tel: (239) 472 1646. Open: 9am–5pm (seasonally – call for details).

McCarthy's Marina

Go dolphin spotting, soak in the sunset, pick up shells or snorkel to your heart's content by joining a boat trip offered by McCarthy's Marina. The most popular tours leave at 10am and return at 3.30pm, allowing two hours of relaxation on nearby Cabbage Key. Alternatively, sunset cruises are just as romantic, but they offer fewer opportunities to explore secret beaches. Day cruises usually include lunch.

Andy Rosse Lane. Tel: (239) 472 5300. www.captivacruises.com

South Seas Resort and Yacht Harbor

This extravagant resort is the place to go for sports and active pursuits. Boasting almost 20 swimming pools, a full golf course and tennis courts, it offers plenty of things to do, albeit at a price. You'll need to be a guest to enjoy the facilities, and rooms start at $200 a night.

Captiva Island. Tel: (239) 472 5111.
www.southseas.com

'Tween Waters Marina

Rent canoes by the hour or by the day at this aquatic activity centre. Tides can be heavy around Captiva, so be sure to ask before you depart in order to plan your route. If you are unsure of your skills, consider joining one of the regular two-hour kayak tours that take in Buck Key.

Captiva Road. Tel: (239) 472 5161.
Open: 7.30am–2.30pm. Rental charge.

You can hire canoes from 'Tween Waters Marina

Tampa and the Gulf Coast resorts

Naples

Laid-back Naples is the place to visit if rest and relaxation are what you desire away from the moneyed masses and celeb-studded crowds of the more exclusive Atlantic resorts. A typical day will usually revolve around a seafood lunch, a round of golf and hours of flopping on the beach, so don't go if luxury living or constant activity are what you demand. Money still exists in these parts, it just isn't as showy as in other areas of the Florida coast.

Children's Museum of Naples

This museum will be the most significant addition to the Naples cultural scene when it opens in autumn 2010. The only museum of its kind in the region, it will feature child-size art studios, mock-up displays of Everglades ecological systems, and an actual beach.

A Banyan tree riddled with cubby-holes acts as the heart of the space, which kids can climb in order to reach a viewing platform at the top of the root and trunk system.

North Naples Regional Park, 15000 Livingston Road. Tel: (239) 514 0084. www.cmon.org. Open: see website for up-to-date information. Admission charge.

Conservancy of Southwest Florida's Naples Nature Center

This wildlife preserve is great for active types thanks to its variety of nature trails and aviaries where you can spot rare bald eagles. Canoe and kayak rentals are also available for more intrepid explorers.

14th Avenue North. Tel: (239) 262 0304. www.conservancy.org. Open: Mon–Sat 9am–4.30pm, Sun 1–5pm. Admission charge.

The rebuilt wooden pier in Naples

Naples Museum of Art

Compared to the larger and more impressive collections at museums on Florida's Atlantic Coast, this small-scale gallery is notable if only for the fact that it is the only one of its kind in the region. The most impressive works fall into two categories: American Modern and Ancient Chinese. Check schedules to see if one of the regular touring exhibits are in town, adding a bit of lustre to the permanent collection.
5833 Pelican Bay Boulevard.
Tel: (239) 597 1900. www.thephil.org.
Open: Tue–Sat 10am–4pm, Sun 2–4pm (Sept–Jul). Admission charge.

Naples Pier

The original pier, built in 1888, was ruined by hurricanes and fire, yet local residents loved strolling its length so much that they have rebuilt it into the glorious promenade that exists today. The pier is open 24 hours but is most popular at dusk when strollers can savour the stunning sunsets.
12th Avenue S at Gulf Coast.

Naples Zoo at Caribbean Gardens

This zoo is actually one of the best in the state thanks to its collection of rare Indochinese tigers, big cats, wild dogs and other exotic creatures, but it doesn't stop there. Especially enjoyable is the multimedia showcase called Safari Canyon, set in a natural rock theatre.
1590 Goodlette-Frank Road.
Tel: (239) 262 5409. www.napleszoo.com.
Open: 9.30am–5.30pm. Admission charge.

Palm Cottage

This 19th-century cottage is the last of its kind in south Florida. Built using tabby mortar – a paste made from burned shells – the home can be toured with guides from the Collier County Historical Society.
137 12th Avenue S. Tel: (239) 261 8164.
Open: Tue–Sat 1–4pm.
Admission by donation.

Palm Cottage, Naples

The northeast

From rockets to race cars and everything in between, the northeast is all about exploration. Here is where you will find the home of Florida's first explorers in the form of the oldest port on the American mainland, St Augustine. Alternatively, follow in the footsteps of today's modern-day explorers, the astronauts who regularly blast off from NASA's Cape Canaveral base, or explore the wonders of Orlando's theme parks.

Not everything is relegated to the history and science books. Cocoa Beach is Florida's surfing capital and no visit is complete without a stop at Ron Jon's Surf Shop – probably the most famous surf shack on the Atlantic Coast. If land-based speed is more to your liking, then Daytona is the place to be with its annual Daytona 500 race, one of the ten most watched sporting events on the planet.

The northeast coast is an area made for speed-freaks and surfers, simple sophistication and solitude. Whether you're a teen looking to kick back on a Spring Break getaway or a more mature traveller in search of five-star frolics on Amelia Island, then this slice of Florida is certain to suit your needs.

CAPE CANAVERAL AND COCOA BEACH

Science, surf and sun are the specialities of the Space Coast, with Cape Canaveral and Cocoa Beach acting as the hub of the region. The highlight of any visit here (if you can time it right) is a space launch, but there is still plenty to see and do if a shuttle isn't going up. Cape Canaveral itself is a prized wetland area with dozens of barrier islands and protected birdlife species. Cocoa Beach, meanwhile, is Florida's best surfing spot, offering great rays and beachside fun.

Astronaut Memorial Planetarium and Observatory

The good news is that this planetarium is the largest of its kind in the state. The bad news is that budget cuts mean that opening hours are now limited to Friday and Saturday nights only. The shows are cutting-edge, with some focusing on teaching visitors about the stars and planets and others with an eye towards laser entertainment.
1519 Clearlake Road. Tel: (321) 433 7373.
www.brevard.cc.fl.us/planet.
Open: Fri & Sat 6.30–10.30pm.
Admission charge.

Brevard Museum of History and Natural Science

Uncover local history by taking a wander through the exhibitions that cover everything from Indian artefacts through to regional insect life. It makes for an interesting two-centre trip when combined with the planetarium (*see opposite*) nearby.

2201 Michigan Avenue. Tel: (321) 632 1830. www.brevardmuseum.org. Open: Tue–Sat 10am–4pm, Sun noon–4pm. Admission charge.

Cocoa Beach Pier

Despite the fact that this pier is more a glorified shopping centre, it remains the most visited attraction in town. The first half of the pier is free of charge and lined with various restaurants and chain stores specialising in goods only a tourist would buy. On weekends there are often performances of live music.

401 Meade Avenue. Tel: (321) 783 7549. www.cocoabeachpier.com. Open: Mon–Thur 9am–10pm, Fri–Sun 9am–11pm.

The northeast

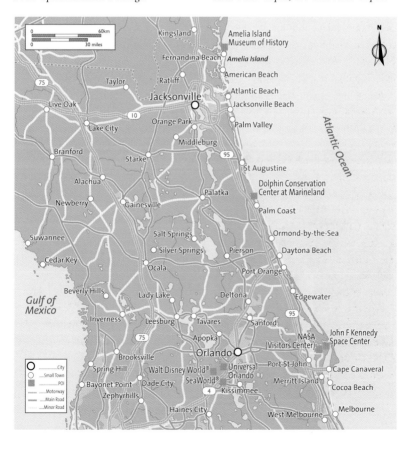

Blast off!

There's nothing like experiencing the roar of the space shuttle as it soars into space to make you value the power of human achievement. Hundreds of astronauts have rocketed into space from Florida's Kennedy Space Center, taking with them the dreams of boys and girls from around the planet to reach for the stars. The sense of excitement in the air when a launch day approaches is palpable. However, delays are common due to poor weather and equipment malfunctions so you may need to prepare yourself for multiple visits if you want to see a launch.

A shuttle on the launchpad at Cape Canaveral

In order to get shuttle launch tickets or check out the upcoming schedule, your first stop should be NASA's official website (*www.ksc.nasa.gov*). Here you can buy launch tickets to the Visitor Complex and get updates on the likelihood of launches occurring. Don't fret if you can't snag an official ticket as there are still plenty of great viewing points off-site, especially on US 1 near the waterfront at Titusville or at the Holiday Inn Riverside-Kennedy Space Center.

Even if a launch isn't scheduled, a visit to the space centre should be on your must-do list. Numerous events in human history began on this site, including the launch of the famous rocket that took Neil Armstrong to the moon and his 'small step for man'.

The first stop for any visitor is the recently renovated and expanded Visitor Center. Be sure to budget a lot of time for your stay as the bus tour takes a minimum of two hours to complete and you can't see the grounds any other way.

Inside the centre, you'll find a plethora of space-related items including actual NASA rockets and a Mission Control room from the

The Rocket Garden at Kennedy Space Center

1960s. Children will adore the hands-on zones that encourage exploration and learning, and there are plenty of opportunities to spend money, including dining areas and space-themed souvenir shops. Freeze-dried ice cream anyone?

For the actual tour, try to go early in the day as the queues to board are almost as long as an actual space mission. Buses depart every ten minutes and it is possible to disembark if you want to spend extra time at any of the destinations en route. Highlight stops include the observation platform with views over the launch pads, the International Space Station Center, and the Astronaut Memorial that bears the names of American astronauts who have died either on a mission or during training. On launch days the bus tours are cancelled so you'll have to make a choice as to whether your priority is to see a launch or enjoy the tour (choose the launch any day!).

If you really want to enjoy a memorable meal, you can have lunch with an astronaut, but you'll need to book well in advance (*Tel: (321) 449 4400*). Alternatively, book yourself onto the Astronaut Training Experience, a unique lecture and experience programme that shows you what astronaut training is like.
Kennedy Space Center NASA Parkway. Tel: (321) 449 4444.
www.kennedyspacecenter.com.
Open: 9am–5.30pm.
Admission charge.

Cocoa Beach Pier at sunset

Florida Solar Energy Center

One for the true science die hards, this research facility has one of the largest libraries and exhibitions dedicated to the study of solar energy. You'll have to book ahead to enjoy a tour as they don't get many visitors, but it's worth it if you have an interest in renewable energy sources.

1679 Clearlake Road.
Tel: (321) 638 1000.
www.fsec.ucf.edu.
Open: Mon–Sat 9am–5pm.
Free admission.

Space Walk of Fame

Honour the work of the astronaut members of the Mercury and Gemini programmes at this centre boasting two monoliths covered with the bronzed handprints of former members. A third monument honouring Apollo astronauts is nearing completion. If a shuttle launch is planned, the walkway offers great viewing opportunities.

Space View Park, Broad Street.
Tel: (321) 264 0434.
www.spacewalkoffame.com.
Open: 10am–5pm.

Valiant Air Command Warbird Air Museum

Plane spotters will be in heaven at this museum that boasts examples of warplanes from throughout the decades. The star attraction is a C-47 built in October 1942 that took part in the Normandy invasion. Other key crafts include the last UH-1 to make it out of Vietnam and an F-14 Tomcat.

6600 Tico Road. Tel: (321) 268 1941.
www.vacwarbirds.org. Open: 10am–6pm.
Admission charge.

DAYTONA BEACH

Daytona Beach has been synonymous with college-kid excess and stock-car racing ever since horseless carriage races were held on the hard-packed sand in the early 1900s. Since that time, the Daytona 500 and alcohol-fuelled Spring Breaks have made the town a popular destination for fans of adrenaline sports and parties that last until the wee hours.

Daytona International Speedway/ DAYTONA USA

Even if you aren't a fan of car racing, a visit to this speedway is a must. The Daytona 500 is what made Daytona Beach famous and the course hosts numerous other racing events throughout the year so there is a good chance something will be going on during your stay. The Daytona 500 is held in February and always sells out so be sure to secure tickets well in advance. When events aren't on, you can test your racing skills on a number of simulators, participate in a pit stop, or pretend you're a radio announcer and 'call' the race on video.
1801 W International Speedway Boulevard. Tel: (800) 748 7867. www.daytonaintlspeedway.com. Open: 9am–7pm. Admission charge.

Halifax Historical Museum

While the displays on-site are very local in aspect, the neoclassical architecture of the former bank in which this museum is housed is worth a look. Exhibits include a number of artefacts used by residents during various periods in Daytona's past and a collection of historic photographs.
252 S Beach Street. Tel: (386) 255 6976. www.halifaxhistorical.org.

Open: Tue–Sat 10am–4pm. Admission charge.

Marine Science Center

Compared to other aquariums and marine research centres in Florida, this one is rather small, with a few indoor exhibits that take a look at various marine habitats such as reefs and mangrove forests. The highlight is a rehabilitation room for sea turtles that examines the effect of harming this endangered species and how further damage can be prevented.
100 Lighthouse Drive, Ponce Inlet. Tel: (386) 304 5545. www.marinesciencecenter.com. Open: Tue–Sat 10am–4pm, Sun noon–4pm. Admission charge.

Museum of Arts and Sciences

For such a trashy resort town, this museum comes as quite a surprise. Best known for its Cuban art collection donated by former dictator Fulgencio Batista, it features a number of interesting works including the only painting made of Argentinian Eva 'Evita' Perón while she was still alive. Other highlights include American and European decorative arts wings, an important collection of Chinese art, a display chronicling Florida history and the largest collection of Ashante gold ornaments in existence.
1040 Museum Boulevard. Tel: (386) 255 0285. www.moas.org. Open: Tue–Fri 9am–4pm, Sat & Sun noon–5pm. Admission charge.

Scandalous Spring Break

Where the boys are! That's what Spring-Breakers say about Florida every February and March when for a single week half of America's college-age kids descend on Florida's party beach. While some love the raucous atmosphere, many locals flee to calmer communities in order to escape the mayhem.

While Daytona has always been a high-adrenaline kind of place – youngsters used to race horseless carriages on the hard-packed sand almost from the day the first Model T rolled off the factory floor – it wasn't always the Spring Break capital. That title fell to Fort Lauderdale until a couple of decades ago when town leaders, sick of the annual disturbance, decided to push the teens out by raising prices and concentrating on higher-priced luxury developments.

Cocoa Beach is a good surfing spot

So what makes Daytona so attractive? First off, it's the price. Daytona's hotel options offer everything from basic rooms in no-star motels to glamorous suites in five-star resorts. Whether you're daddy's little princess or a hard-up scholarship student, you're bound to be able to afford a stay. Additionally, domestic flights are now extremely cheap and it's well situated on the Interstate system for drivers.

Secondly, it's the wealth of activities. College kids like to play by day and drink by night. During the sunlight hours, holidaymakers can swim, sail, water-ski, jet-ski, dive, race and snorkel to their heart's content. If that's not enough, there's also surfing in nearby Cocoa Beach and the near-constant array of parties put on by such companies as MTV. Trying to secure a poolside dance platform on network television is considered the holy grail of many a college girl's career. Additionally, local bars take a somewhat relaxed approach to the legal drinking age, with many a fake ID getting plenty of mileage.

Finally, there's a sense of history. On many campuses Daytona is spoken of with a kind of reverence. Undergraduates have older sisters, brothers, uncles, aunts, cousins and even parents who speak of their time here as almost mystical in quality. A more sober stay might make them

The crowds of students attract top international artists to Daytona

realise they are rose-tinting their memories, as the plethora of cheap T-shirt shops and souvenir stands does much to mar the landscape. Despite this, it's still a great place for a spot of people-watching.

Due to the immense width of the beach, Daytona is one of the few beaches where driving along the coast is absolutely legal, except in locations where sea turtles are nesting. Be sure to watch for signs, as fines are huge for those who ignore the warnings. A cruise along the boardwalk by car is a nightly ritual for many a student, but not to admire the sunset. Rather, this is how you check out the opposite sex and impress with your wheels. Those with souped-up motors always get preferential treatment, especially if the person driving it is just as attractive.

Ponce de Leon Inlet Lighthouse and Museum

This lighthouse is the second tallest in America. Built in the 1880s, it has since been restored and now holds a variety of exhibits that cover everything from lighthouse operations to nautical history. While the view from the top is stunning, the trek up the 203 steps can be a killer so take your time while ascending.

4931 S Peninsula Drive. Tel: (386) 761 1821. www.ponceinlet.org. Open: 10am–9pm (late May–early Sept); 10am–5pm (mid-Sept–mid-May). Admission charge.

ST AUGUSTINE

The oldest permanent European settlement in the United States is this port, which was founded in 1562.

Castillo de San Marcos, St Augustine

Looking more like a European town with its Spanish-style architecture, tiny lanes and cobbles, it's an atmospheric place with a long history dating back to the days of Ponce de León (who first sighted the Florida coast in 1513 and claimed the land for Spain). The sites listed in this section are worthy of exploration, while the highlights of St Augustine can be discovered on the walk through its historic streets (*see pp102–3*).

Authentic Old Jail

Prisoners of the county were holed up in this historic jail from its construction in 1890 until 1953. The sheriff would live above the cells with his wife and children, using the same kitchen to prepare family meals and inmate requests. It isn't huge, but it's certainly atmospheric and speaks of a time when crime meant the gallows and solitary confinement.

The jail is also home to the **Florida Heritage Museum**, a mostly rag-tag collection that uses artefacts from the past to tell the story of Florida's history. Specific focus is placed on the life and times of Henry Flagler, the Civil War and the Seminoles.

167 San Marco Avenue. Tel: (904) 829 3800. Open: 8.30am–5pm. Admission charge.

Dolphin Conservation Center at Marineland

Listed on the National Register of Historic Places, this once-tacky aquatic park is now a scientifically advanced centre used to study our aquatic friends. Dolphins, sharks and penguins are on display – reserve in advance and you can even swim in the tanks with them!

9600 Ocean Shore Boulevard.
Tel: (904) 460 1275.
www.marineland.net. Open: Wed–Mon 9.30am–4.30pm. Admission charge.

Old Florida Museum

This museum tells the story of Florida's history through the use of hands-on exhibits. Find out about historical eating and farming practices by actually doing it! Most of the exhibits are outdoors, so it's not the best place to go on a rainy day.

254D San Marco Avenue.
Tel: (904) 824 8874.
www.oldfloridamuseum.com.
Open: 10am–5pm. Admission charge.

St Augustine Alligator Farm and Zoological Park

For over a century, this gator park has been drawing in the crowds to see its collection of reptiles, including a number of rare, white crocs. It is the only place in the world that houses all 22 species of crocodilians – over 2,700 animals in total. There are also a number of regional birds, marshes in which they can enjoy wading, a petting zoo and reptile shows throughout the day.

999 Anastasia Boulevard.
Tel: (904) 824 3337.

St Augustine Alligator Farm houses all known crocodile species

www.alligatorfarm.com.
Open: 9am–5pm. Admission charge.

World Golf Village

You have to really like golf in order to appreciate the trappings of this centre offering shops and hotels dedicated to the sport. There is an IMAX theatre showing golf movies, shops where you can buy golf supplies, a number of 18-hole championship golf courses and the *pièce de résistance,* the World Golf Hall of Fame.

21 World Golf Place. Tel: (904) 940 4000.
www.wgv.com. Open: varies per activity – see website for details.
Admission charge.

Walk: In search of the Fountain of Youth

Ponce de León stumbled on the area around St Augustine during his search for the Fountain of Youth. You may not be able to locate the mysterious water source on your walk, but you can certainly enjoy the journey through some interesting history.

This walk of around 2¼ miles (3.5km) will take approximately 4 hours.

Begin your trip down memory lane at the corner of St Francis and Charlotte.

1 The Oldest House

Dating back to between 1702 and 1727, this home is the oldest in town.
14 St Francis Street. Tel: (904) 824 2872. www.staugustinehistoricalsociety.org. Open: 9am–5pm. Admission charge. Go north on Charlotte and then turn left on Bridge Street.

2 Dow Museum of Historic Houses

Ten restored homes re-create life from the Spanish colonial era to modern day.
250 St George Street. Tel: (904) 823 9722. Open: 9am–4.30pm. Admission charge. Continue along Bridge Street and then turn right onto Cordova.

3 Lightner Museum

Once an opulent hotel, this museum houses one of the best collections of Victoriana in the country.
75 King Street. Tel: (904) 824 2874.

www.lightnermuseum.org. Open: 9am–5pm. Admission charge. Turn right onto King until you reach Aviles.

4 Spanish Military Hospital

See how the Spanish were cured at this reconstruction of a hospital that stood here from 1784–1821.
3 Aviles Street. Tel: (904) 827 0807. www.spanishmilitaryhospital.com. Open: Mon–Sat 10am–5pm, Sun noon–5pm. Admission charge. Go back to St George Street and then go north to just beyond Curia Street.

5 Colonial Spanish Quarter

Costumed actors re-create 18th-century life during the Spanish colonial period.
33 St George Street. Tel: (904) 825 6830. www.historicstaugustine.com. Open: 9am–5.30pm. Admission charge. Continue north on St George Street.

6 The Oldest Wooden Schoolhouse

Classes were held here until 1864.
14 St George Street. Tel: (904) 824 0192.

www.oldestwoodenschoolhouse.com.
Open: 9am–5pm. Admission charge.
Continue north on St George and then
turn right onto Orange.

7 Castillo de San Marcos National Monument

This fort is the oldest and best
preserved in America.
1 E Castillo Drive. Tel: (904) 829 6506.
www.nps.gov/casa. Open:
8.45am–4.45pm. Admission charge.
Continue on S Castillo to Ocean.

8 Mission of Nombre de Dios

The first permanent US mission.
27 Ocean Avenue. Tel: (904) 824 2809.
Open: 8am–5.30pm. Free admission.
Go back to San Marco and turn right on
to Myrtle, then left on Magnolia.

9 Fountain of Youth Archaeological Park

Evidence points to the existence of
a Timucuan Indian Village 1,000
years ago.
Backtrack to San Marco and head south.

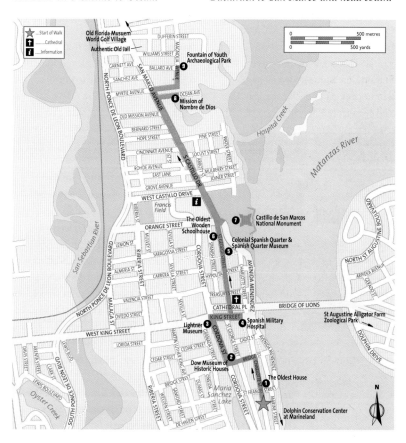

JACKSONVILLE

Miami might have the bigger name, but Jacksonville is actually the biggest city in the state. With a large African-American population and predominantly blue-collar background, Jacksonville has a reputation as an industrial town, but banking and insurance industries have moved in, bringing money to the region. The metropolis is now slowly regenerating, offering numerous diversions for those willing to scratch its surface.

Cummer Museum of Art and Gardens

Visual art is celebrated in this museum housed in a Tudor-style mansion within lush grounds. Works span the centuries from 2000 BC to today, with

A fountain at the Cummer Gardens

highlights including some fine French Impressionist works and Japanese woodblock prints. The grounds are especially beautiful, with both English-and Italian-style gardens.
829 Riverside Avenue. Tel: (904) 356 6857. www.cummer.org. Open: Tue & Thur 10am–9pm, Wed & Fri–Sat 10am–5pm, Sun noon–5pm. Admission charge.

Jacksonville Landing

Dining, clubbing, live music and performance can all be found at this popular shopping and entertainment complex on the north bank of the St Johns River. Not just for tourists, it's also a popular place for locals looking for a great night on the town.
2 Independent Drive. Tel: (904) 353 1188. www.jacksonvillelanding.com. Open: Mon–Thur 10am–8pm, Fri & Sat 10am–9pm, Sun noon–5.30pm.

Jacksonville Zoo and Gardens

This 73-acre (30-hectare) park is considered the best zoo in the southeast due to its ever-growing collection of exotic species and great exhibitions about local flora and fauna. Vast in size, a visit can easily fill the day, so take advantage of the stroller and wheelchair rentals if you think toes might get tired during your stay. A 2$^{1}/_{2}$-acre (1-hectare) Kids' Zone is great for helping tots let off steam in the splash pools, mazes and climbing frames.
8605 Zoo Parkway. Tel: (904) 757 4462. www.jaxzoo.org. Open: 9am–5pm. Admission charge.

MOCA Jacksonville

Just like the Getty Museum in Los Angeles, bigger doesn't always mean better. Both this museum, built in 2003, and the Getty suffer from the same thing: a lack of world-renowned art. Without years of collecting to fall back on, the MOCA has to make do with the rare masterpieces that come onto the market. Despite this, there is still much to impress the casual visitor as some great works by Joan Mitchell and James Rosenquist are housed here in addition to well-equipped educational studios and interpretive centres.

333 N Laura Street. Tel: (904) 366 6911. www.mocajacksonville.org. Open: Tue & Thur–Sun 10am–4pm, Wed 10am–9pm. Admission charge.

Ritz Theater and LaVilla Museum

Between 1921 and 1971, the LaVilla neighbourhood was considered Black America's southern capital, fostering the growth of numerous prominent names in the African-American community. Many famous performers began their careers at the Ritz before heading north to the more accepting clubs above the Mason-Dixon line. Try to snag tickets to a show or, failing that, go into the LaVilla Museum to find out more about local African-American culture.

829 N Davis Street. Tel: (904) 632 5555. www.ritzlavilla.org. Open: Tue–Fri 10am–6pm, Sat 10am–2pm, Sun 2–5pm. Admission charge.

Jacksonville's skyline

AMELIA ISLAND

Located almost smack-bang on the Georgia border, Amelia Island is Florida's northernmost barrier island. Located a 45-minute drive northeast of Jacksonville, the island boasts a delightful collection of Victorian residences and holds an important place in America's black history.

During the 1930s, Amelia Island was the only place African-Americans in the United States could holiday due to strict segregation laws that prevented them from mixing on Florida's white-only shores. Thousands of heat-starved blacks from America's northern states would flock down each winter in order to enjoy the beaches, restaurants and hotels of the area, including many nightclubs that played host to jazz legends like Duke Ellington, Count Basie and Ella Fitzgerald.

Traditional architecture in Fernandina Beach

Americans during the years of segregation. At one point, this beach was the only one open to African-Americans in the entire state and northern black workers flocked to its shores to enjoy hotels, restaurants and clubs owned by fellow members of America's African-American community. As desegregation became law, Amelia Island lost popularity as holidaymakers chose destinations closer to home.

Amelia Island Museum of History

Once the town jail, this museum is Florida's only such building dedicated to the preservation of oral history, an important historical tool in chronicling African-American history. Displays include overviews of the history of various island industries and a photographic record of the effects of tourism on the community. The best way to enjoy the museum is to go on the regular 'eight flags' tour held at 11am and 2pm every day, which covers the eight flags that have been raised over the island, from the French flag in 1562 to the American flag after the end of the Civil War.
233 S 3rd Street. Tel: (904) 261 7378.
www.ameliaislandmuseumofhistory.org.
Open: Mon–Sat 10am–4pm.
Admission charge.

American Beach

The heart of Amelia Island is this beach, once home to a thriving community of vacationing African-

Fernandina Beach

Located in the middle of Amelia Island is this residential town boasting a collection of restored Victorian, Italianate and Queen Anne-style homes, of which many are listed on the National Register of Historic Places. If you are a fan of architecture, then this community is sure to delight.
Fernandina Beach.

Fort Clinch State Park

Built in 1847, Fort Clinch never saw battle but has served as a base for the armed forces throughout many wartime periods including the Civil War and World War II. Advancements in weaponry made the fort obsolete almost from the moment the building was completed. See how troops lived at a re-enactment of the evacuation of Confederate forces, performed during the first weekend of every month.
Fort Clinch. Tel: (904) 277 7274.
www.floridastateparks.org/fortclinch.
Open: 8am–sunset. Admission charge.

ORLANDO

Without a doubt, Orlando is best known for its theme parks, including the Walt Disney World® Resort, Universal Orlando and SeaWorld®. However, this region is also home to hundreds of smaller, family-friendly attractions, plus outdoor activities, shopping opportunities, restaurants for casual and fine dining, sports and culture. Before Disney built and opened the Disney World® Resort back in 1971, the Orlando area mostly consisted of farmland, orange groves and wilderness. Today, it has become one of the most visited holiday destinations in the world.

The region where the theme parks and tourist attractions are located is typically referred to as the 'Orlando area'. It encompasses Orlando, Kissimmee and Lake Buena Vista.

Orlando's arts and cultural scene

Beyond the popular theme parks, there is plenty to see, do and experience in the Orlando area. The arts and cultural activities are typically located closer to Downtown (about a 30-minute drive from the theme parks).

Harry P Leu Botanical Gardens

This laid-back and non-commercial attraction is a great alternative to the busy theme parks. Take a quiet, self-guided tour through lush gardens featuring beautiful flowers and exotic plants. Exhibits change throughout the seasons. Check the website for special programmes, outdoor concerts and guided tour availability.
1920 North Forest Avenue, Orlando.
Tel: (407) 246 2620. www.leugardens.org.
Open: daily 9am–5pm. Admission charge (but free Mon 9am–noon).

Orlando Ballet

Many visitors are surprised by the superior quality of the productions offered by this professional ballet company. Shows change throughout the year.
1111 N Orange Avenue, Orlando.
Tel: (407) 426 1739.
www.orlandoballet.org. Show schedule varies throughout the year.
Admission charge.

Harry P Leu Botanical Gardens

Orlando Museum of Art

If you appreciate ancient or contemporary American art, you will enjoy Orlando's most respected art museum. Permanent collections also include African art. Additional visiting exhibits, with varied themes, are also showcased throughout the year.
2416 North Mills Avenue, Orlando.
Tel: (407) 896 4231. www.omart.org.
Open: Tue–Fri 10am–4pm, Sat–Sun noon–4pm. Closed: Mon and public holidays. Admission charge.

Orlando Philharmonic Orchestra

Christopher Wilkins leads this award-winning orchestra, offering formal evenings of music and culture. A wide range of performances are presented year-round.
Bob Carr Performing Arts Centre,
401 West Livingston Street, Orlando.
Tel: (407) 896 6700 or 770 0071
(box office). www.orlandophil.org.
Show schedule varies throughout the year; box office is open Mon–Fri 9am–5pm. Ticket prices vary based on performance.

Orlando Science Center

At this interactive museum, suitable for the entire family, you'll encounter a range of exhibits and special events designed to entertain and educate. The CineDome offers a unique movie experience on a massive eight-storey-high screen.
777 E Princeton Street, Orlando.
Tel: (407) 514 2000 or (800) OSC 4FUN. www.osc.org. Open: daily

CityWalk is the permanent Orlando home for Blue Man Group

10am–5pm (Sat until 10pm). Closed: Easter, Thanksgiving & Christmas. Admission charge.

Orlando Shakespeare Theater

This professional theatre company presents an ongoing line-up of Shakespeare's most beloved works. In 2010, *Hamlet* and *All's Well that Ends Well* are among the scheduled offerings. This troupe also presents shows for a younger audience, including Schoolhouse Rock Live in March and April 2010.
812 E Rollins Street, Loch Haven Park.
Tel: (407) 447 1700.
www.orlandoshakes.org. Box office open: Mon–Fri 10am–5pm, and one hour prior to show times. Ticket prices vary by performance.

Shows

The following are not your typical Broadway-style theatrical productions. They are, however, presented once or twice a night, and are all family-orientated entertainment experiences that in some cases include a multi-course dinner.

Arabian Nights Dinner Show This fun-filled interactive dinner show features beautiful horses, knights and plenty of adventure.
3081 Arabian Nights Boulevard, Kissimmee. Tel: (407) 239 9223. www.arabian-nights.com.
Admission charge includes dinner.

Blue Man Group Featuring a cast of talented musicians covered in blue make-up, Blue Man Group represents a new form of entertaining performance art, complete with very unusual instruments and off-beat humour.
Sharp AQUOS Theatre, CityWalk, 600 Universal Boulevard, Orlando. Tel: (407) 224 3200. www.blueman.com.
Admission charge; discounts are offered with Universal Orlando theme park ticket purchases.

Cirque du Soleil La Nouba Clowns, acrobats and a variety of non-traditional circus performers are featured in this Cirque du Soleil show. The music, choreography, colourful costumes and unusual acts are all breathtaking and memorable.
Downtown Disney®, 1478 E Buena Vista Drive, Lake Buena Vista. Tel: (407) 939 7328. www.cirquedusoleil.com/lanouba.
Admission charge.

Medieval Times Dinner Show A light-hearted, interactive dinner show featuring horses, knights and comedy.

See alligators up close when you take a high-speed ride in an airboat

4510 W Irlo Bronson Highway,
Kissimmee.
Tel: (866) 543 9637.
www.medievaltimes.com.
Admission charge includes dinner.

Pirates Dinner Adventure
Swashbuckling action, pirate
mayhem and comedy are combined
in this entertaining and whimsical
dinner show.
6400 Carrier Drive, Orlando.
Tel: (800) 866 2469.
www.piratesdinneradventure.com.
Admission charge includes dinner.

**Wonder Works, The Outta Control
Magic Comedy Dinner Show** Stand-up
comedy combined with magic and
plenty of audience participation.
Dinner includes unlimited pizza.
9067 International Drive, Orlando.
Tel: (407) 351 8800.

Fantasy of Flight is a relatively new attraction in
the Orlando area

www.wonderworksonline.com.
Admission charge includes dinner.

Popular attractions on International Drive and beyond

Boggy Creek Airboat Rides
A family-friendly attraction that will
take you gliding along in an airboat.
You are guaranteed to see live alligators
up close and in the wild.
2001 E Southport Road, Kissimmee.
Tel: (407) 344 9550.
www.bcairboats.com. Open:
9am–5.30pm. Admission charge.

Fantasy of Flight
This family-owned airfield features
working aeroplanes from throughout
the history of aviation. Air shows are
presented regularly and guests can
experience a biplane or hot air balloon
ride for an additional fee.
1400 Broadway Boulevard SE,
Polk City. Tel: (863) 984 3500.
www.fantasyofflight.com.
Open: daily 10am–5pm.
Admission charge.

Gatorland
Gatorland brings visitors up close to
hundreds of alligators and crocodiles.
Spend at least three to five hours
enjoying the self-paced exhibits,
along with the interactive shows.
The alligator wrestling show should
not be missed.
14501 South Orange Blossom Trail,
Orlando. Tel: (407) 855 5496.
www.gatorland.com. Open: daily at

Experience the thrill of being a NASCAR driver as you race around a professional track

9am; closing time varies by season. Admission charge.

Orlando Hot Air Balloon Rides

Take a romantic, early morning hot air balloon ride over Orlando and the surrounding area. Experience spectacular views from hundreds of feet in the air as the sun rises and you find yourself gliding with the wind in a colourful balloon. Your adventure ends with a champagne toast.

Take-off locations vary, based on weather. Tel: (800) 586 1884 or (407) 894 5040. www.orlandoballoonrides.com. Open: daily flights at sunrise. Admission charge.

Richard Petty Driving Experience

Imagine what it is like driving at ultra-fast speeds in an actual NASCAR racing car on a professional track – that's the experience offered at Richard Petty Driving Experience. Full training and equipment is included; if you opt not to drive, you can experience a less expensive ride-along with a professional driver.

Walt Disney World® Speedway, 3450 N World Drive, Lake Buena Vista. Tel: (800) 237 3889. www.1800bepetty.com. Open: daily, hours vary by season. Admission charge.

Ripley's Believe It or Not!®

This museum offers hundreds of unusual, strange and sometimes grotesque exhibits. Anyone over the age of ten will enjoy what's offered here. *8201 International Drive, Orlando. Tel: (407) 363 4418. www.ripleysorlando.com. Open: daily 9.30am–midnight. Admission charge.*

SkyVenture Orlando Indoor Skydiving

Jump out of an aeroplane and skydive, but without wearing a parachute or risking your life; you are never more than a dozen feet (4m) off the ground.

At SkyVenture, visitors experience indoor skydiving

This is a totally safe indoor skydiving experience for those aged 12 and over that includes all of the equipment and instruction needed for an exciting 'flight' in a massive wind tunnel that simulates a free fall. Including training, the whole thing lasts about an hour.
6805 Visitors Circle, Orlando (across from Wet 'n Wild®).
Tel: (407) 903 1150 or (800) 759 3861.
www.skyventureorlando.com. Open: Sun–Thur 11.30am–9pm, Fri–Sat 11.30am–10pm (reservations required).
Admission charge.

Wet 'n Wild®
This independent water park has been around for years and offers a full day's worth of pools, water slides and other outdoor activities. Towels and lockers are available to hire.
6200 International Drive, Orlando.
Tel: (407) 351 1800 or (800) 992 9453.
www.wetnwildorlando.com.
Open: varies by season.
Admission charge.

Wonder Works
This highly unusual indoor theme park offers virtual reality rides, hands-on activities, unique exhibits and a wide range of experiences for all ages.
9067 International Drive, Orlando.
Tel: (407) 351 8800.
www.wonderworksonline.com.
Open: daily 9am–midnight.
Admission charge.

The Walt Disney World® Resort
The Walt Disney World® Resort, set on 40sq miles (104sq km) of land in Lake Buena Vista, comprises 4 massive theme parks (Disney's Animal Kingdom®, Disney's Hollywood Studios™, Epcot® and The Magic Kingdom®), 2 water parks, 33 resort hotels, 6 timeshare properties, 81 holes of championship golf, 2 full-service day spas, the Disney's Wide World of Sports® complex, the Walt Disney World® Speedway (race track), the Downtown Disney® shopping area, hundreds of restaurants and many other activities and attractions.

The key to experiencing the best possible holiday here is to pre-plan your time at the theme parks and determine, in advance, which rides, shows and

attractions you are most interested in. You should also take full advantage of the FastPass programme (*see box, p115*) to help avoid long queues for popular attractions.
Tel: (407) W-DISNEY.
http://disneyworld.disney.go.com

Disney's Animal Kingdom®
By creatively combining live animal shows and exhibits with Disney-style rides, shows and attractions, Disney's Animal Kingdom® (*http://*

GOLF IN ORLANDO

Orlando has become a premier destination for avid golfers, thanks to the growing number of public courses and luxurious golf resorts in the region. The Walt Disney World® Resort is home to five of its own championship courses – Eagle Pines (18 holes), Magnolia (18 holes), Oak Trail (9 holes), Palm (18 holes) and Osprey Ridge (18 holes).
Tel: (407) 939 4653.
www.disneyworldgolf.com
  Nearby Celebration (the town designed by Walt Disney himself) also has an 18-hole championship course (*tel: (407) 566 465; www.celebrationgolf.com*) and a golf academy. Other notable golf resorts in the area include **Ginn Reunion Resort** (*tel: (407) 396 3180; www.reunionresort.com/golf/golf.asp*), which has three 18-hole courses, designed by Arnold Palmer, Jack Nicklaus and Tom Watson. There's also the **Rosen Shingle Creek Golf Club** (*tel: (407) 996 9933; http://shinglecreekgolf.com*), plus the upscale **Ritz-Carlton Golf Club** (*tel: (407) 393 4906; www.ritzcarlton.com*), which features an 18-hole course designed by Greg Norman.
Tee times and rates vary by season at each course. Equipment rentals are available. Reservations are always required.

---

disneyworld.disney.go.com/parks/animal-kingdom) is one of the world's more unusual theme park experiences. The main attraction here is Kilimanjaro Safaris, which is an open vehicle adventure through an African-style savannah. While accompanied by a guide, you will get close to real-life giraffes, gazelles, elephants, rhino, lions and dozens of other animals living in their natural habitats. Each tour lasts 20 to 30 minutes, and they run throughout the day.

  The Pangani Forest Exploration Trail is a walking adventure featuring dozens more wild animal exhibits. Young explorers in particular will enjoy the Wildlife Express Train to Rafiki's Planet Watch – a series of educational and entertaining animal shows and exhibits that includes a petting zoo, called Affection Section. Apart from the real-life animal attractions, some of your favourite Disney characters can be seen daily in the Animal Kingdom's popular Jammin' Jungle parade.

DINOSAUR A turbulent, fast-moving thrill ride that takes visitors on a time travel adventure to see dinosaurs. Not suitable for young people under 40in (102cm) tall.
Expedition Everest-Legend of the Forbidden Mountain This indoor/outdoor, state-of-the-art roller coaster offers teenaged and adult adventurers a high-speed ride around and through Mount Everest, where the Abominable Snowman awaits.

Riders must be at least 44in (112cm) tall.

Festival of the Lion King A live, theatre-in-the-round musical show featuring costumed characters, singers, dancers and acrobats who retell Disney's *The Lion King*.

Finding Nemo – The Musical Utilising larger-than-life puppets, special effects and extremely talented performers, Disney's *Finding Nemo* comes to life in this visually stunning show.

Flights of Wonder This live show features skilled animal trainers and a collection of exotic birds. It's a family-friendly show that's presented throughout the day.

It's Tough to Be a Bug! Anyone over the age of six will enjoy this light-hearted, somewhat educational, but highly enjoyable 3-D movie that is based on Disney's *A Bug's Life*.

Kali River Rapids You'll probably get soaked as you experience this white water rafting adventure that takes you along a turbulent artificial river. Riders must be at least 38in (97cm) tall.

Disney's Hollywood Studios™
With a behind-the-scenes look at television and film, Disney's Hollywood Studios™ (*http://disneyworld.disney.go. com/parks/hollywood-studios*) offers a combination of production shows, rides, interactive attractions, exhibits, restaurants and shops. Families can easily spend one to three full days exploring this theme park.

Disney's Hollywood Studios™ has recently undergone expansion and alteration, with new things to see and do, including:

American Idol Experience The newest interactive show at this theme park is based on US television's most popular talent competition, *American Idol*. Every morning, visitors audition to participate in live shows that are held throughout the day. The shows last about 45 minutes each, but you'll want to arrive at least 30 minutes early to ensure a seat in the massive theatre. The American Idol Experience is suitable for all ages, but you must be aged 14 or over to audition and perform.

Beauty and the Beast – Live On Stage This 30-minute live show features actors and costumed characters retelling the story of Disney's animated classic.

Fantasmic! Combining music, animation, special effects, lasers, costumed characters, incredible fireworks and synchronised shooting water, Fantasmic! is truly a breathtaking and original show that should not be missed. The 25-minute show is presented nightly after dark.

High School Musical 3: Right Here! Right Now! Ideal for younger children and teenagers, songs and music from Disney's *High School Musical 3* are presented in a high-energy, well-choreographed, concert-like show.

Muppet-Vision 3D Featuring Kermit the Frog, Miss Piggy and the rest of

WALT DISNEY WORLD® THEME PARK TICKET PRICES

At the time of writing, adult ticket prices range from $75 for a one-day pass to $237 for a ten-day pass. Child ticket prices range from $63 to $202. There are also some optional add-ons:

- an extra $50 to gain admission to the water parks
- a 'no expiration date' option costing $17–200 (depending on the number of days), which ensures that your tickets don't expire after their usual 14-day limit
- a $50 'park hopper' feature, allowing you to visit more than one theme park in a day.

Parking costs $12 per day.

Separate admission fees apply to Typhoon Lagoon, Blizzard Beach (both $40/$34) and Disney's Wide World of Sports® ($11/$9).

FastPass

To avoid waiting in long queues (30–90 minutes) for each popular Disney theme park attraction, take advantage of the free FastPass service available at the entrance, which gives guests a specific time period to return to each attraction in order to experience it without a wait.

Jim Henson's classic Muppet characters, this is an entertaining and funny 3-D movie.

Playhouse Disney – Live On Stage This live show features characters, music and stories based on the popular *Playhouse Disney* television shows.

Rock 'n' Roller Coaster Starring Aerosmith This is an indoor, high-speed, extremely turbulent roller coaster that features loud music from rock band Aerosmith and special effects. Riders must be at least 48in (122cm) tall.

Toy Story Midway Mania Experience colourful scenes and characters from Disney's *Toy Story* in this 4-D adventure movie and ride.

The Twilight Zone Tower of Terror Not for the timid, this ride features stunning special effects as guests explore a haunted hotel. The ride ends with a sudden 13-storey free fall that repeats multiple times. Not suitable for people less than 40in (102cm) tall.

Voyage of the Little Mermaid With special effects and larger-than-life puppets, this live show retells Disney's *The Little Mermaid* in a heart-warming and visually impressive way.

Epcot®

Designed to be both educational and fun, primarily for teenagers and adults, Epcot® (*http://disneyworld. disney.go.com/parks/epcot*) is really two distinct theme parks in one.

Within **Future World**, you'll find nine separate pavilions that offer fun-filled rides, shows and attractions. As you enter Epcot® from the main entrance, the giant, golf ball-shaped structure is home to a slow-moving ride called Spaceship Earth that explores the history of communication. The Universe of Energy is a 45-minute ride and movie that showcases all of the different energy sources available. Over at Test Track, visitors receive a first-hand look at how General Motors tests its vehicles for safety and durability. This is one of Epcot's two thrill rides, and is not suitable for young children.

The Imagination! Pavilion takes visitors on a journey into their own creative minds through hands-on activities, a 3-D movie and a slow-moving musical ride. The Seas offers interactive shows plus massive aquariums featuring real-life exotic creatures from the ocean. The Seas with Nemo & Friends is a light-hearted ride featuring characters from Disney's *Finding Nemo* movie.

The Mission: Space Pavilion features the most thrilling ride in this theme park. Suitable for teenagers and adults, this is a true spaceship simulator, which is the closest thing riders can get to experiencing a real-life rocket launch without becoming an astronaut. The Land Pavilion is where you'll find Soarin', a simulator ride that takes passengers on a hang-glider journey around California. Riders must be at least 40in (102cm) tall. Inside Innovations you'll find a variety of ever-changing, hands-on exhibits that showcase current and up-and-coming technologies.

Surrounding a large artificial lake, the **World Showcase** area of Epcot® includes a number of pavilions that represent countries from around the world, including Mexico, Norway, China, Germany, Italy, the USA, Japan, Morocco, France, the UK and Canada. Each one is staffed by natives of their respective countries and features rides, shows, attractions, shops and authentic casual and fine dining experiences.

Exploring all of Epcot® could easily take one to two full days (or longer), and requires a significant amount of walking from pavilion to pavilion.

The Magic Kingdom®

The Magic Kingdom® (*http://disneyworld.disney.go.com/parks/magic-kingdom*) was Disney's first theme park here in Orlando, and of all the Disney parks, it is the most child-friendly. One favourite activity is to dine with the Disney characters for breakfast or lunch (an additional fee applies). Be sure to make advance reservations for Cinderella's Royal Table.

While adults can explore the 142 acres (57ha) of The Magic Kingdom® in around a half day or full day, depending on crowds, if you're travelling with children you should plan on spending between one and two full days here. Opening hours vary throughout the year, but crowds tend to thin out during peak meal times, during the parades and late in the day.

Big Thunder Mountain Railroad

Climb aboard this runaway railway for a fast-paced adventure through a deserted mine. Not suitable for those under 40in (102cm) tall.

The Haunted Mansion Guests exploring Liberty Square ride in slow-moving chairs through this seemingly old mansion. Special effects are used to create the many ghosts who haunt the building.

It's a Small World An indoor, musical boat voyage featuring animatronic characters depicting children from around the world singing the classic *It's a Small World* song.

Mad Tea Party This classic ride allows passengers to spin around and around in giant tea cups. Not suitable for very young children.

The Many Adventures of Winnie the Pooh This ride retells the story of Winnie the Pooh, with visitors travelling through a giant storybook.

Mickey's County House You are guaranteed to meet Mickey Mouse here for a great photo opportunity, but be prepared for a wait.

Mickey's PhilharMagic A wonderful 3-D movie featuring Disney's classic characters and eye-popping special effects.

Pirates of the Caribbean This is a slow-moving boat ride originally created by Walt Disney himself, which has since been updated to feature characters from the Disney films.

Space Mountain This famous indoor roller coaster sends passengers on a simulated space flight. Riders must be at least 44in (112cm) tall.

Splash Mountain Follow the adventures of Brer Rabbit in this light-hearted boat ride that ends with a five-storey plummet and a huge splash (not suitable for young children, and yes, you will get wet).

Presented each day within The Magic Kingdom® is a musical character parade featuring many of Disney's best-loved characters. In the evening, don't miss an additional parade that ends with a fantastic fireworks display atop Cinderella's castle (*parade times vary*). The best vantage points to see the parades and fireworks are along Main Street USA.

When entering any of the Disney theme parks, be sure to pick up a free, full-colour Guide Map, plus a separate show and character meet and greet schedule. In the centre of The Magic Kingdom®, near the statue of Walt Disney and Mickey Mouse, is a Tip Board which displays current waiting times for all of the rides and attractions within the park.

Other Disney World activities and attractions

Blizzard Beach and Typhoon Lagoon water parks Families can easily spend entire days enjoying the slides, pools and other water-based activities on offer. Separate admission tickets are required.

Celebration, Florida This is a real-life town that Walt Disney himself designed. Utterly charming, the Main Street area offers shops, restaurants and cafés, plus a lake where paddle boats and fishing gear can be hired. Celebration also has a boutique hotel and a championship golf course.

DisneyQuest An indoor, high-tech theme park offering virtual reality simulators, state-of-the-art video games, and dozens of interactive activities. A separate admission ticket is required.

Disney's Wide World of Sports® This 220-acre (89ha) sports complex allows guests to participate in popular sports, and watch and interact with professional athletes.

Downtown Disney®/Disney's West Side More than 24 one-of-a-kind shops, the world's largest Disney Store and themed restaurants. Open every day until at least 10pm (and usually much later).

Universal Orlando theme parks

Originally, Universal Orlando was a working film studio and theme park modelled after its Hollywood counterpart. However, over the years it has expanded into an entertainment complex that many believe rivals Walt Disney World®.

The Universal Orlando complex includes the Universal Studios Florida theme park, the Islands of Adventure theme park and CityWalk.
6000 Universal Boulevard, Orlando.
Tel: (407) 363 8000.
www.universalorlando.com

CityWalk

Located between Universal Studios and Islands of Adventure is CityWalk (*www. universalorlando.com/citywalk.html*), a massive entertainment, dining and

The grand entrance to Universal Orlando

shopping complex that is open daily between 11am and 2am. There are themed hotels, including the **Loews Portofino Bay Hotel** (*Tel: (407) 503 1000*), the **Hard Rock Hotel** (*Tel: (407) 503 7625*) and the **Loews Royal Pacific Resort** (*Tel: (407) 503 3000*). After dark, for a flat fee, you can gain unlimited access to all of the nightclubs within CityWalk, where you can dance, drink and karaoke the night away. Live music is presented free on the CityWalk main stage, but you will find live entertainment within the clubs and restaurants, too (*separate admission fees may apply*). CityWalk is also where you will find the theatre where Blue Man Group (*see p109*) performs one or two shows nightly (*additional admission fee applies*).

CityWalk offers many themed restaurants that are family-friendly, including the world's largest Hard Rock Cafe, the NASCAR Sports Grille, Emeril's Restaurant, NBA City and The Bubba Gump Shrimp Company. Shopping and a massive 20-screen AMC cinema round out CityWalk's offerings.

Islands of Adventure

Islands of Adventure (*www.universalorlando.com/amusement-parks/islands-of-adventure.html*) is all about thrill rides with a theme. This park is home to multiple roller coasters, plus an assortment of other rides and attractions that will keep your adrenalin pumping.

The Simpsons Ride puts you into an adventure featuring characters from the TV series

In Seuss Landing you will find a handful of rides and attractions based on Dr Seuss' books and characters. The Cat in the Hat ride is probably the most impressive and shouldn't be missed. Within The Lost Continent area, you'll find The Dueling Dragons – a massive two-track roller coaster – plus a handful of other rides and attractions.

The Jurassic Park area is based on the hit films and takes you to a place where life-size dinosaurs roam freely. The Jurassic Park River Adventure is the main ride here. It ends with an up-close encounter with a life-size T-Rex and a massive drop. Over in Toon Lagoon, the fun is more light-hearted and offers plenty of water-based action. Dudley Do-Right's Ripsaw Falls is a wild and wet flume ride that ends with an incredible splash (you will get wet).

Comic book fans will love Marvel Super Hero Island. The Amazing

Adventures of Spider-Man is a motion simulator ride that offers incredible and life-like special effects, while Doctor Doom's Freefall drops you from 150ft (46m) in the air. The Incredible Hulk is this park's flagship roller coaster. In 2010, The Wizarding World of Harry Potter, one of the most anticipated theme park attractions ever, will open. This massive area will allow visitors to become part of Harry Potter's magical world – for a preview, visit www.universalorlando.com/harrypotter

Throughout the day, visitors can meet popular costumed characters – check the free Adventure Guide for times and locations.

This larger-than-life monolith marks the entrance to Islands of Adventure

Universal Studios Florida

The underlying theme at Universal Studios Florida (www.universalorlando.com/theme-parks/universal-studios-orlando/hours.html) is TV and film. If you're travelling with children, be sure to check out the Animal Actors on Location live show featuring famous animals from TV shows and films performing tricks, along with the A Day in the Park with Barney show, which brings this popular TV character to life. Fievel's Playland, ET Adventure and Jimmy Neutron's Nicktoon Blast are among the other attractions for children.

Throughout the day, costumed characters interact with visitors within the park. Check the free studio map and guide for meet and greet times and locations.

Hollywood Rip Ride Rockit The newest thrill ride at Universal Studios is this fast-moving (65mph/105kph) roller coaster that takes you on an airborne ride around the theme park.

The world's largest Hard Rock Cafe at CityWalk is loaded with rock 'n' roll memorabilia that you can admire as you dine

Jaws While you enjoy a slow-moving boat ride through Amity, a Great White shark lurks in the waters surrounding this small village. Not suitable for young children.

Men In Black Alien Attack Based on the *Men In Black* movies, you take on the role of an MIB agent in training, shooting aliens with a laser gun.

Shrek 4-D Meet Shrek, Donkey and Princess Fiona in this 3-D movie with a 4-D twist. The theatre is interactive, so audience members become truly immersed in the story.

The Simpsons Ride The newest interactive ride at Universal Studios is also its best. This motion simulator ride takes you through an exciting and action-packed tour of Krustyland. Of course, you will encounter all of your favourite animated characters from *The Simpsons*. Riders must be at least 40in (102cm) tall.

Terminator 2: 3-D An original 3-D movie based on the *Terminator 2* film. May be too scary for young children.

Twister…Ride It Out You would never want to be caught in the middle of a real-life tornado, but this attraction allows you to see what it would feel like first-hand.

SeaWorld® Resorts
SeaWorld® offers three theme parks (SeaWorld®, Discovery Cove and Aquatica) with up-close encounters, shows and exhibits showcasing exotic marine life, such as killer whales,

Orlando's newest and most impressive water park, Aquatica

dolphins, penguins, sea lions and sharks. You'll also discover a handful of thrill rides and roller coasters.
7007 SeaWorld Drive, Orlando. Tel: (800) 327 2324. www. seaworldorlando.com. Open: varies throughout the season, visit www. seaworld.com/ParkHours.aspx for details.

Aquatica

Aquatica (*www.aquaticabyseaworld.com*) is the newest water park in Orlando and SeaWorld's answer to Disney's Typhoon Lagoon and Blizzard Beach. This massive park features over a dozen different water rides, plus wave pools, swimming pools, massive artificial beaches and a meandering, lazy river.

Intertwined with the various rides are aquatic animal exhibits, so for example as visitors experience the Dolphin Plunge (a giant water slide), they will travel through a pool inhabited by dolphins. There are rides, slides and activities for people of all ages.

Discovery Cove

Discovery Cove (*www.discoverycove. com*) offers both entertaining and educational encounters with a wide range of exotic sea creatures and birds. For a limited number of visitors each day, this is a full-day experience. The highlight includes swimming with bottlenose dolphins and snorkelling in an artificial reef with stingrays.

All of the equipment and instruction you will need throughout the day is provided as part of this highly personalised and memorable experience – just bring a swimsuit. Marine life experts and trainers are available to interact with guests and answer questions. The Discovery Cove experience isn't cheap, but it is unique and only available to 1,000 people per day, so advance reservations are required.

SeaWorld®

Each year, SeaWorld® (*www. seaworld.com/orlando*) continues to expand. While the flagship show at SeaWorld® continues to be Believe (the heart-warming killer whale show presented within Shamu Stadium), there are now also numerous thrill rides and other live shows, plus unique animal exhibits.

The newest ride within SeaWorld® is Manta, a roller coaster that simulates a fast-paced ride through underwater worlds. Riders are strapped onto the belly of a giant, 12ft (3.5m) manta ray that takes them on a whirlwind journey through the park as they spin, glide, skim and soar their way through up-close animal encounters.

A'Lure, The Call of the Ocean This is an innovative live show that features acrobats and dancers, all wearing colourful costumes. The show is presented multiple times throughout the day.

Blue Horizons (Whale and Dolphin Theatre) See dolphins, birds and other marine creatures perform tricks. Shows are presented throughout the day.

Dolphin Cove Interact with dozens of dolphins and feed them raw fish (an additional fee applies for feeding).

Kraken SeaWorld's most popular roller coaster takes the form of a mythological sea monster. Not suitable for young children.

Manatee Rescue This is a live animal exhibit where trainers and experts are on hand to answer questions about these gentle, giant sea creatures.

Mistify Fireworks and Fountain Spectacular Every evening after dark, enjoy a breathtaking fireworks and synchronised fountain water show, complete with special effects. It is an impressive show for the entire family.

SEAWORLD® THEME PARK TICKET PRICES

At the time of writing, adult ticket prices range from $75 for a one-park, two-visits ticket to $329 for admission to all three parks. Child ticket prices range from $65 to $329.

Discounts for advance online ticket purchases are offered; visit *www.seaworld.com*

The Orlando Flex Ticket offers discounted admission to SeaWorld®, Aquatica, Universal Studios Florida, Islands of Adventure and Wet 'n Wild® for $235 (adult) and $214 (child).

Penguin Encounter This indoor attraction stars hundreds of penguins swimming, sliding and playing in their natural habitat. It is suitable for all ages.

Shark Encounter From the world's largest underwater viewing tunnel you will get a close look at dozens of sharks, moray eels, barracudas and other sea creatures. Suitable for all ages.

Believe at SeaWorld®, starring a cast of killer whales and their trainers

The Panhandle

Stretching across the north of the state is Florida's Panhandle, a collection of towns that often have more in common with the genteel South. Here, you will find planned communities, plantations, rowdy resorts and unspoiled beaches all within a few miles of each other. It's also the location of the state capital of Tallahassee, a sleepy southern city that lives and dies by state politics and the fortunes of its hometown Florida State University Seminoles football team.

Of all the regions of Florida, the Panhandle is the least visited by international travellers due to the area's lack of big-name sights. You won't find any large-scale amusement centres or big-city trappings beckoning to holidaymakers in these parts. Instead, a drive to the communities that line Interstate 10 and the north Gulf Coast reveals quaint culture in Pensacola, the 'redneck' Riviera of Panama City and one of the most challenging hiking trails in the South through Apalachicola National Forest. It may not feature a lot of flash and dazzle, but for those searching for pristine beauty and unparalleled natural vistas, the Panhandle is the place to head for. This is where the 'real' Florida exists – one of sand, sea, surf and sun.

Tallahassee

For the state that boasts the Latin beats of Miami, the redneck kitsch of Panama City, space exploration and Orlando's thrills, the state capital comes as a bit of a shock. Tallahassee has more in common with the sleepy Southern towns of Georgia, Alabama and Mississippi than it does with Florida, and this is reflected in the antebellum architecture and canopy roads that give the region a languid beauty.

Black Archives Research Center and Museum

Philanthropist Andrew Carnegie built the library in which this extensive collection of African-American history and artefacts is housed.
Florida A&M University, Martin Luther King Jr Boulevard at Gamble Street.
Tel: (850) 599 3020.
www.famu.edu.
Open: Mon–Fri 9am–4pm.
Free admission.

Capitol complex

Tallahassee's Capitol building became a common sight during the 'hanging chad' news coverage that occurred following the 2000 presidential elections. The New Capitol with its modern skyscraper is much less appealing visually than the domes of the Old Capitol, yet boasts amazing views from the top. Also on the complex site is the Vietnam Veterans Memorial and Governor's Mansion.

Monroe Street at Apalachee Parkway. Tel: (850) 488 6167. Open: Mon–Fri 8am–5pm. Free admission.

Knott House Museum

Built by a free African-American builder in 1843, this Victorian home was the location of Florida's first reading of the Emancipation Proclamation in 1865.

301 E Park Avenue. Tel: (850) 922 2459. www.taltrust.org/knott.htm. Open: Wed–Fri 1–4pm, Sat 10am–4pm. Admission charge.

Maclay Gardens State Park

The northern financier Alfred Maclay began planting this 300-acre (120-hectare) ornamental garden for the delight of the public back in 1923. Today, it is alive with over 200 bloom varieties and dotted with nature trails, lakes, boating and canoe rental huts and more.

3540 Thomasville Road. Tel: (850) 487 4556. Open: 9am–5pm. Admission charge for cyclists and vehicles only.

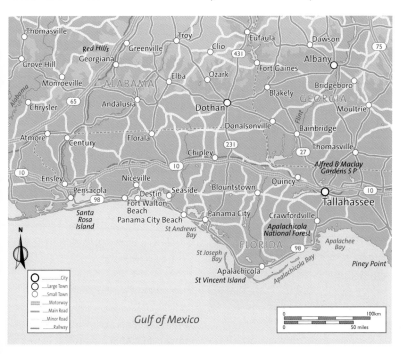

Tailgate parties and college football

In order to understand exactly what a tailgate party is, you have to comprehend the power that American football has on Florida (and the South in general). For many small towns in the Southern United States, football is a religion that pulls more worshippers to its pews every week than the local church. The reason? Both religion and football offer the keys to pearly gates leading to heaven.

High-school students play football to become college students that play football. Most stop there, having achieved their dream of a university education gained on full scholarship, but a lucky few continue to the big-time in the form of the NFL.

College football games are fiercely competitive with some stadiums holding just as many fans in the bleachers as you would find at big city arenas. And surrounding all the hoopla of game day is the tailgate party, a beer-fuelled, bbq-powered celebration by fans as they get ready for the match.

On match day, alumni and supporters arrive early, sometimes many hours in advance, to set up. Deckchairs come out, coolers are filled with ice, radios are switched on and spaces are demarcated in the car park. Friends and family then congregate around the tailgate of a car to fill up on picnic food items like coleslaw and potato salad as the countdown to kick-off commences.

By far the biggest tailgate parties occur on homecoming weekend when alumni of a university come home for a weekend in October to get back in touch with old friends. This is always the hardest ticket to snag during the season and tailgate parties can be wild. Many who don't have a ticket go to the lot just to join in the tailgate fun.

Sometimes the football is secondary to the party

A typical tailgate party at a Miami–Boston game

Florida State University, with its perennial contenders the Seminoles, is one of the better-known college football teams. It's under the direction of coach Bobby Bowden, who has run the team for over 30 years. Bobby is considered a celebrity in Tallahassee and his image is used on billboards and ads throughout town. Bowden can boast an extremely successful record, having placed college football teams in the top five for fourteen years in a row between 1987 and 2000 (although recent years have not been so successful). The main rival for the 'Noles' are the University of Florida Gators, playing out of their home in Gainesville. Games between the two teams are some of the most fiercely fought in the country and tickets on match days between the two at Doak Campbell Stadium are like gold dust.

If you plan on joining the fun, be warned that drink-driving is a regular problem and police officers watch vehicles as they leave for any signs of erratic behaviour. Whatever you do, don't mix beer with pleasure, and leave plenty of time between your last drink and your first trip behind the wheel.

To check schedules or book tickets to a Seminole game, telephone (*Tel: (850) 644 1830*) or check out their website (*www.seminoles.com*). It's a good idea to check the match times whether you're interested in football or not, as the city grinds to a halt whenever a match is in progress.

Drive: Canopy roads of Tallahassee

Tallahassee sometimes seems like a city that lives in its past due to the volume of antebellum-style homes that line the streets of its outskirts. While it's the capital of Florida, it feels more like a sleepy Southern town than a political powerhouse. The best way to explore the city's past is by car along the canopy roads, lanes lined with trees – usually pines and oaks – covered in Spanish moss and forming a kind of canopy.

Begin your journey at the site of the Old Capitol Building on Monroe Street at Apalachee Parkway. This tour can take a half or full day depending on how long you decide to drive along each road.

1 The Old State Capitol

While it's no longer the site of government, the Old Capitol is still the symbolic home of political power in this city that honours its past just as

The Old State Capitol

much as it controls the state's future. Built in 1845, the building has since been restored to its former glory. An exhibition inside takes a look at the history of the state's politics – weirdly neglecting the 'hanging chad' dilemma that eventually resulted in the selection of President Bush in 2000. A visitor centre in the New Capitol offers driving maps of the canopy roads.

Take Monroe Street north to the junction of Old Bainbridge Road and turn left.

2 Old Bainbridge Road

Old Bainbridge Road is considered the best of the canopy roads and should be the one you drive if you are short of time. It leads to Havana, a town known for its art galleries and handicraft stores.

If you want to see more canopy roads, backtrack from Havana and then go east once you reach the I-10 until you hit Meridian Road.

3 Meridian Road

The second canopy road on the tour is this lane that keeps on going until it reaches the Georgia border. Turn back here to see more architectural and natural wonders.

Reach the next road by backtracking to the I-10 and then turning right onto Capital Circle. Turn left at the next major intersection you come to.

4 Centerville Road

If you're going on to Jacksonville, consider taking this road as a more picturesque alternative.

To get to the next road, backtrack along Centerville and then turn left onto Capital Circle. Take another left at the next major intersection.

5 Miccosukee Road

This picturesque road passes through hardwood and pine forests, home to over 46 species of birds.

Backtrack along Miccosukee and then turn left on Capital Circle. Turn left for the final canopy road onto Old St Augustine Road.

6 Old St Augustine Road

The final canopy road, and the only one that goes south. Take this drive for a little way if you plan to go towards Gainesville and points in central Florida.

Alternatively, return to where you started by turning back on Old St Augustine, cross over Capital Circle, then follow the Apalachee Parkway before turning left on Monroe.

Drive: Canopy roads of Tallahassee

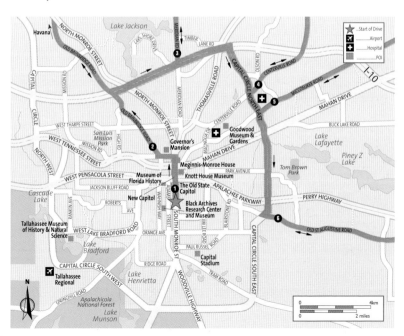

Meginnis-Monroe House
Enjoy fine arts in the surroundings of this antebellum home that dates from 1852. Local artists' works are put on display in the various rooms, including pieces by Jacques Lemoyne, a French artist sent to Florida in 1564 and widely considered to be the first European artist to depict Florida on canvas.
125 N Gadsden Street.

Tel: (850) 222 8800. www.lemoyne.org. Open: Tue–Sat 10am–5pm, Sun 1–5pm. Closed: Mon. Admission charge.

Mission San Luis de Apalachee
Built in 1656, this was the chief mission complex in northwestern Florida until 1704. The goal was for the Franciscan monks to convert the local Apalachee Indians to Catholicism. The buildings

The quiet end of Panama City Beach

have since been restored using research and archaeological digs.

2021 Mission Road. Tel: (850) 487 3711. www.missionsanluis.org. Open: Tue–Sun 10am–4pm. Closed: Mon. Free admission.

Museum of Florida History

From 10,000 BC to today, the history of the great state is chronicled in this museum that looks at prehistory, native tribes and European influence and discovery in equal measure.

R A Gray Building, 500 S Bronough Street. Tel: (850) 245 6400. www.museumoffloridahistory.com. Open: Mon–Fri 9am–4.30pm, Sat 10am–4.30pm, Sun noon–4.30pm. Free admission.

Panama City Beach

Sunshine seekers from across the South flock to this value-packed beach resort that caters to a raucous clientele. Amusement parks, thrill rides and wax museums are the name of the game here. Surprisingly, it's also the location of some of Florida's most unspoiled beaches. Stick to town for in-your-face fun or drive just a little way outside to see Florida as it was meant to be.

Gulf World Marine Park

Kids love this place, but adults may be less thrilled by the variety of trained animal shows on offer. Parrots, penguins, dolphins and more all perform daily, with shark feedings and underwater shows filling in the gaps.

A 'trainer for a day' programme and dolphin swimming encounters are available for an extra charge.

15412 Front Beach Road. Tel: (850) 234 5271. www.gulfworldmarinepark.com. Open: daily 9am–4pm (summer); 9am–2pm (rest of the year). Admission charge.

Museum of Man in the Sea

Did you know that people have been underwater diving since 1500? If not, then this museum dedicated to the history of diving and sunken treasure will put you right. Displays examine air pressure and light refraction to explain how diving works.

17314 Panama City Beach Parkway. Tel: (850) 235 4101. www.maninthesea.org. Open: daily 10am–4pm. Admission charge.

St Andrews State Park

You might think that Florida's beaches are a mess of condos, suntanned teens, raucous rebels and souped-up vehicles. Restore your faith by going to this state park and experiencing the 1,000 acres (405 hectares) of sand dunes and powder-soft grains beneath your feet. Only here can you feel like Robinson Crusoe as you wander along the trails, picnic in public grounds, fish in shallow waters and pick wild rosemary.

4607 State Park Lane. Tel: (850) 233 5140. www.floridastateparks.org/standrews. Open: daily 8am–sunset. Admission charge for cyclists and vehicles only.

The Panhandle

Cities that work

Those who argue that planned communities are an American thing have never been to the UK's Milton Keynes, yet the planned communities of Florida are so American in look and feel that it's no wonder visitors find the idea of them so foreign. The most famous manufactured town is the hamlet of Seaside, located to the east of Destin in Florida's Panhandle. Avid movie-goers may recognise the town as the location for the film *The Truman Show* starring Jim Carrey.

If you're just stopping for a few moments, a visit may make you feel slightly bemused as the entire community seems so fake in its desire to create something so authentic. Faux Victorian touches have been added to modern homes to give them a lived-in and romantic look, and a strictly imposed pastel and white colour scheme has been rigorously adhered to by all citizens. Some find the overall result quaint, beautiful and highly liveable, while others find the whole thing claustrophobic and bland.

Seaside came into existence during the 1980s as a concept following the 'New Urbanist' architectural movement. At the time of its construction, there were no zoning ordinances for the area, giving the builders free rein to create a community to their exact specifications. Ironically, while the town was modelled on diverse communities in more urban centres such as New York and San Francisco, the end result has been the formation of a mostly white, upper-middle-class village that largely shuns the socio-economic integration of other centres.

While it isn't a gated community, Seaside is seen by outsiders as a gated town due to its homogeneous population. Many also feel that this is a construction reaction to the high crime rates that plagued Florida during much of the 1980s.

The town's influence has been strong; other New Urbanist centres – such as Disney's Celebration near Epcot® – have developed in reaction to Seaside's success. Business development has been limited as the majority of residents live here only part-time, with most of the focus on service-industry jobs such as in shops and restaurants to cater to the wealthy clientele.

As Seaside grows, it is developing more character, and many artists, writers and creative types are moving

Seaside's houses have a Victorian look about them

in. Despite the fact that homes and buildings allow for no self-expression, the calm surroundings appeal to creatives in search of a restful location from which they can develop their crafts.

Overseeing the town is the Seaside Institute, a research foundation established by Seaside's original founder, Robert Davis. The institute serves to respond to the ever-changing needs of the town and its residents by constantly analysing global trends in order to enhance everyday life. Regular forums on architecture and town planning are held here, making it an essential stop for students of urban planning or for those simply intrigued by the idea of how to build a town from the ground up, so to speak.

To reach Seaside, take scenic highway 30-A west for about 20 miles (32km) from Panama City Beach.

Shipwreck Island Water Park

This water-based fun park has slides, wave pools and rivers galore in which to cool down. For young kids there is a Tad Pole Hole with gentler options. *12201 Middle Beach Road. Tel: (850) 234 3333. www.shipwreckisland.com. Open: Jun–Jul daily 10.30am–5.30pm; Apr–May & Aug–Sept, times vary – call for details. Admission charge.*

ZooWorld Zoological and Botanical Park

Smaller than most of the other state zoos, the focus here is on endangered species and the protection of the most challenged of the lot. To see how they do it, be sure to go to the Infant Care Facility to see the zoo's most recent additions. *9008 Front Beach Road. Tel: (850) 230 1243. www.zooworldpcb.net. Open: daily 9am–5.30pm. Admission charge.*

Victorian home in Pensacola

Pensacola

Called the City of Five Flags due to the five flags that have flown over it since its founding, Pensacola offers something for everyone. A vast naval base entices military buffs, historic architecture is like honey to cultural bees, while nearby beaches such as Pensacola Beach and the Gulf Islands National Seashore offer incredible corners on which to stop and savour the sunshine and birdlife.

Historic Pensacola Village

Experience Pensacola's past in this collection of buildings, all of which are listed on the National Register of Historic Landmarks. During the summer, costumed actors go about re-enacting life as it was in yesteryear. Highlights include the Black History Museum, Christ Church and the Museums of Commerce and Industry. *205 E Zaragosa Street. Tel: (850) 595 5985. www.historicpensacola.org. Open: Mon–Fri 10am–4pm. Admission charge.*

National Museum of Naval Aviation

Depending on your view of war, this museum will either inspire or appal you. Over 100 aircraft are on display in addition to a number of exhibits that portray naval and marine life in all its glory. Simulator rides provide a taste of what it's like to fly a jet fighter while other rooms take a look at the life of POWs. Glossy it may be, but there are still areas that focus on the rough edges of the military.

Julee Cottage is part of Historic Pensacola Village

US Naval Air Station, Radford Boulevard. Tel: (850) 452 3604. www.naval-air.org. Open: 9am–5pm. Free admission.

Northwest Florida Zoological Park and Botanical Gardens

Bring the kids to this well-stocked zoo boasting over 700 species including most of the 'Big Five' of Lion, Buffalo, Leopard, Elephant and Rhino. If you need to rest your feet, the Safari Line train runs past free-ranging herds through 30 acres (12 hectares) of preserve land. Alternatively, take advantage of this rare opportunity to see a Komodo dragon in the new Dragon World area.

5701 Gulf Breeze Parkway. Tel: (850) 932 2229. www.thezoonorthwestflorida.org. Open: 9am–5pm. Admission charge.

Palafox Historic District

Enjoy a stroll along Palafox Street from the water's edge to Wright Street to take in the glorious Spanish- and Mediterranean-inspired architecture of the central business district of Pensacola. One highlight is the Saenger Theatre with its ornate exteriors. Florida became a state in 1821 in this district when General Andrew Jackson accepted it into the United States.

Palafox Street between the water's edge and Wright Street.

Pensacola Historical Museum

Pensacola has one of the more interesting histories of all the towns in Florida due to its 'Five Flags' past. This museum examines Pensacola in great detail. Don't miss the dig of a Spanish army compound operated by the museum across the street.

115 E Zaragosa Street. Tel: (850) 433 1559. www.pensacolahistory.org. Open: Mon–Sat 10am–4.30pm. Admission charge.

Pensacola Museum of Art

The works at this former jail are pretty minor but are worth checking out if you have an interest in decorative glass or American Moderns. Regular events are often surprisingly fun, especially the Art After Dark programmes, which encourage you to explore your own creativity.

407 S Jefferson Street. Tel: (850) 432 6247. www.pensacolamuseumofart.org. Open: Tue–Fri 10am–5pm, Sat & Sun noon–5pm. Admission charge.

Getting away from it all

Too often the natural wonders of Florida are ignored in favour of the shopping centres and thrill rides of the state's major resorts. Florida's national and state parks are just an hour or two away from the hustle and bustle of city life – some featuring environments, flora and fauna that are completely distinct to the region. The Everglades should be top of everyone's list as global warming threatens this delicate ecosystem.

Apalachicola National Forest

The southern half of the state generates the biggest buzz when it comes to wildlife preserves and national parks. To focus all the attention there, however, is to ignore one of Florida's most pristine natural green spaces in the form of the Panhandle's Apalachicola National Forest. Residents of the state capital visit frequently, as easy access from Tallahassee means that a day trip (or even a one-hour jaunt) is perfectly feasible. Silver Lake, Lost Lake and Trout Point offer great camping and picnic facilities, but you might want to consider going even further into the forest to witness more secluded and unspoiled surroundings.

The 500,000 acres (202,000ha) that make up the forest feature a diverse range of topographies including swampland and savannas with nature trails liberally scattered throughout. Cutting through the forest is the Ochlockonee River, which flows south towards the gulf feeding the various lakes and swamps. While highways do cut through the region, most roads are not paved, so a four-wheel-drive vehicle is recommended if you plan on any back-country exploration.

Should you require any assistance or guidance during your stay, drop by one of the ranger stations. If you're in the west, then head over to **Apalachicola Ranger Station** (*Tel: (850) 643 2282*) and south to the town of Bristol close to where Highways 12 and 20 meet. In the east, the **Wakulla Ranger Station** (*Tel: (850) 926 3561*) is in Crawfordville off Highway 319.

The biggest challenge (and the one that gives the greatest rewards) is the 30-mile (48km) Apalachicola Trail, which begins its journey just off US 319 near Crawfordville. This trek should be undertaken only by serious hikers. Ample water and food supplies should be brought in the event of emergency as some stretches are extremely isolated and there are no refreshment spots en route. Try not to go during or immediately after a rain shower as water levels in some of the swamps can rise fast around the Bradwell Bay Wilderness region, which can make for slow (and extremely damp) going. At the end of the trail is Camel Lake, a well-maintained camping ground with clean toilets and fresh drinking water available.

If you want to undertake a trail walk but are daunted by the idea of a 30-mile (48km) trek then consider instead the 9-mile (14.5km) Camel Lake Loop Trail, reachable by taking Highway 20 to Bristol and then driving a further 12 miles (19km) south.

Worth making a side trip for is the **Fort Gadsden Historic Site**, the location of an early 19th-century British fort that housed both Native and African-American soldiers trained to battle the Spanish during their fight for control of the state. During the Civil War, it then housed Confederate soldiers in an ironic twist of fate. The fort can be reached by taking Highway 65 to Forest Road 129 and then driving west until you go south on Forest Road 129B.

Apalachicola National Forest can be reached from Tallahassee by taking Highway 319 south to Crawfordville or Highway 20 east from Panama City Beach. Open: daily 8am–sunset. Day use fee.

Bald cypress trees at low water

Corkscrew Swamp Sanctuary

Birdwatchers consider the state of Florida to be a dream destination due to the sheer variety of species that can be found dotted across the region. The best location in which to enjoy a birdwatching holiday is arguably the National Audubon Society property located in the Corkscrew Swamp Sanctuary. The sheer number of birds that call this 11,000-acre (4,450-hectare) preserve home is sometimes overwhelming – birds absolutely adore the area due to the flawless condition of the swamps and forests. A visit here can feel as though you've just been cast as an extra in *Jurassic Park* thanks to the lush greenery that seems to speak of the primeval.

At the last count, there were over 100 species of birds visible within the park's confines in addition to alligators, otters, turtles and Florida black bears. In the middle of it all is a 2¼-mile (3.6km) boardwalk trail through a forest of bald cypresses where it may seem as though you are the last person on the planet as you listen to the sounds that swirl around you.

Corkscrew Swamp is actually surrounded by the Big Cypress National Preserve, a protected wilderness area that was declared after uncontrolled logging decimated much of the region, destroying thousands of 500-year-old trees. Wood storks that nested high in the limbs of these towering trees were

A baby alligator at Corkscrew Swamp

The gorgeous plumage of the blue heron

brought to the brink of extinction and are only now just beginning to bounce back in numbers. Corkscrew Swamp can now safely claim to house the largest population in the country.

Despite the fact that the preserve can be tricky to reach due to its remote location, the end result is worth the aggravation. A prevalence of mosquito fish in the area's waters means that there are relatively few mosquitoes bothering you during your explorations, as their larvae are considered a fantastic meal by these incredibly resourceful aquatic residents.

Be sure to stop off at the visitor centre to pick up the self-guided tour booklet that provides copious information about the boardwalk trail and the various flora and fauna you might see during your stay. As all the animals have different peaks in terms of activity throughout the day, avid

wildlife lovers may want to arrange for multiple visits at different hours to witness different species.

If you can, try to visit during the dry season. Between November and April summer rains can drench the preserve with very little notice, and with the towering trees putting everything into shade, it can feel surprisingly cool and humid following a severe storm. Disabled visitors and those with small children should note that the boardwalk is level and easily manoeuvrable. Wheelchairs and strollers are available free of charge at the Blair Visitor Center at the main gate.

Corkscrew Swamp is located between Naples and Fort Myers. Follow Interstate 75 to exit 17 and then go east on Highway 846. Tel: (239) 348 9151. www.corkscrew.audubon.org. Open: Oct–Apr 7am–5.30pm; May–Sept 7am–7.30pm. Admission charge.

Airboat in a canal off Alligator Alley

Everglades National Park

Think of the Everglades and the first image that comes to mind is of a big swamp – 1.5 million acres (607,000 hectares) of it to be exact. Wet and murky it might be, but it is also Florida's most important ecosystem where numerous endangered species find safe haven away from the encroaching development of the rest of the state. The best way to see the region is by using airboats. These zippy vehicles are great for getting through the saw grass in a timely manner, but they don't allow you inside the actual park as they are banned within its borders. From the deck, it's possible to see alligators, leatherback turtles, bald eagles, manatees and the elusive Florida panther.

To get inside Everglades National Park, you can choose to enter from either the north or the east. The northern entrances offer the more scenic routes while the southern entrances will help you reach your destination faster.

There are a number of visitor centres at the park that can help you arrange a worthwhile trip, but the best for general questions is the **Everglades National Park Headquarters** in Homestead (*Tel: (305) 242 7700*). An alternative is the **Ernest F Coe Visitor Center** at the park headquarters entrance west of Homestead (*Open: 8am–5pm*). Boat rental and tour details are posted at the visitor centre and the on-site staff offer plenty of tips and advice.

One of the best things to do during a visit is to follow one of the well-marked trails that run through the park. The most popular is Shark Valley, a 15-mile (24km) route of paved road that is loved by cyclists. While it doesn't offer the best viewing, its popularity lies in its easy access from the Tamiami Trail, the main two-lane stretch of road that cuts across south Florida from Miami to the Gulf Coast along the northern border of the Everglades.

Walkers and hikers will prefer the Gumbo Limbo Trail, a $^1/_2$-mile (0.8km) trail that begins about 3 miles (5km) from the main entrance of the park. This is the best journey to take if you are interested in plant life, as it guides you past fine examples of orchids, ferns, palms, trees and more. Right next to the Gumbo Limbo is the Anhinga Trail, which is known more for its wildlife, specifically alligators, otters, native birds and reptiles.

Less active types may want to consider joining a tour. Tram tours of Shark Valley are available at the Shark Valley entrance, taking two hours to complete the journey. All tours are led by a qualified naturalist and stop at a 65ft (20m) observation tower that offers amazing views over the park. Book via telephone (*Tel: (305) 221 8455*) or website (*www.sharkvalleytramtours.com*). *Take the Tamiami Trail west from Miami or east from Naples to the northern entrances around Shark Valley or southwest from Miami on the Florida Turnpike to Florida City, where you can then follow Palm Drive to the Ernest F Coe Visitor Center. 40001 State Road 9336, Homestead. Tel: (305) 242 7700. www.nps.gov/ever. Admission charge for vehicles and bicycles only.*

A dragonfly perches in the Everglades

When to go

Florida is a great place to visit year-round thanks to near-constant warm weather and tropical sunshine. Between May and November the hurricane season sets in, but even during wet weather days there are still plenty of things to see and do. In fact, if the rain is a light drizzle, the day can turn out to be perfect for major sites such as Busch Gardens as queues drop significantly for the big rides.

Peak and low seasons

Peak seasons (and subsequently peak rates) vary from region to region. In south Florida, high season occurs in the winter from December to April. Prices during this period can as much as double, so consider travelling during the shoulder periods of May and November if you want good weather and better bargains. In the summer, the heat and humidity can be tiresome but hotels offer significant discounts.

North Florida experiences the reverse, with summer drawing the crowds and winter providing the deals.

Orlando gets extremely busy during school and most public holidays, especially between Thanksgiving (fourth Thursday in November) and New Year (1 January). Theme park crowds are at their heaviest during these periods, which means longer queuing times for the popular attractions. During July and August Orlando becomes hot and muggy, which makes it less comfortable to be outside.

Hurricane watch

Hurricane season lasts from mid-May to November. If you are in Florida when a warning occurs, read the *Miami Herald* online (*www.miamiherald.com*) for updates. Hurricanes are devastating tropical storms – you just have to look at the effect Katrina had on New Orleans to see how much damage they can do. If a hurricane is approaching your resort, try to get out of town. If that's not an option, move as far away from the coast as possible and search for higher ground. For more details on hurricanes, see the 'Hurricane hotspots' feature (*pp48–9*).

Holidays

School holidays draw crowds across the state regardless of the weather. You may think travelling to south Florida in August will translate into cheap rates, but you'll find that hotels go down in cost with flights rising in price due to demand. You're best to go to package operators for holidays during this season, as negotiated discount airfares may translate into savings.

Locally, crowds are affected by American holiday dates, especially at major tourist attractions and theme parks. For a full list of Florida's holiday dates, see p168.

Climate
Spring
Warm weather hits around mid-March, bringing tropical storms. The season lasts until about May, by which time the state is covered in greenery.

Summer
The humidity rises during summer, which runs from May to September. Inland, the heat can become unbearable; on the coast, breezes provide welcome relief. Lightning storms and downpours are frequent during this period, usually hitting in the afternoon.

Autumn
Considered by many to be the best time to visit Florida, September to November offers cooler and drier conditions.

Winter
Bring an extra layer as the temperature can drop at night. Typical daytime temperatures hover around 70°F (21°C).

WEATHER CONVERSION CHART

25.4mm = 1 inch

°F = 1.8 × °C + 32

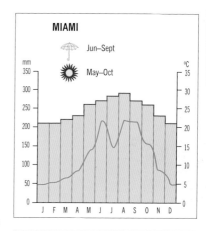

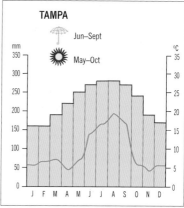

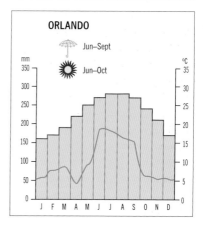

Getting around

Florida owes its tourism prosperity to transportation, as it wasn't until Henry Flagler built the Atlantic Coast railway that visitors from the north began taking the idea of a holiday in America's tropics seriously.

Today, the state's comprehensive interstate and highway system means that almost every corner is accessible. Watch out for traffic jams on weekends when it may seem as though the entire state has come out to play.

By train

The romance of the rails can still be experienced on one of two routes operated by Amtrak, America's passenger train carrier. Along the Atlantic Coast, the Silver Meteor and Silver Star run from New York City down to Miami or Tampa stopping at Atlantic coastal towns along the way. The entire journey lasts about 26 hours. Alternatively, take the Sunset Limited from Los Angeles to Orlando, with stops in Pensacola and Tallahassee (68 hours). Bookings for both routes can be made through **Amtrak** (*Tel: (800) 872 7245. www.amtrak.com*).

Miami's Metrorail train line runs from Palmetto, north of the airport, through the city to Dadeland, south of the university. There is also a free monorail service downtown.

The Walt Disney World® Monorail System transports guests between The Magic Kingdom®, Epcot® and a handful of the Disney resort hotels.

By car

Florida's highway system is efficient and easy to use. Foreigners renting a car will find the state set up for their convenience, as international driving licences are not required unless your home nation does not print the licence in English.

Speed limits are 65mph (105km/h) or 70mph (112km/h) on rural interstate highways. You will probably find yourself driving well below the posted limits, but on highways that run through urban areas or have fewer lanes, traffic may be even slower.

Every major car rental firm has representation in Florida. Competition is stiff, so you will often find that there are deals to be had during slow seasons.

In order to rent a car in Florida, you must be aged 25 or older and have a valid credit card. Some firms will rent to you if you are 21, but you will pay a premium.

Alamo
Tel: (800) 327 9633. www.goalamo.com

Avis

Tel: (800) 331 1212. www.avis.com

Budget

Tel: (800) 527 0700. www.budget.com

Hertz

Tel: (800) 654 3131. www.hertz.com

Thrifty

Tel: (800) 367 2277. www.thrifty.com

By plane

Orlando International Airport (MCO) and Miami International Airport (MIA) are the two busiest points of entry. Continental, US Airways and Delta all operate commuter services throughout the state through their small-scale partners.

Of all the resort destinations in Florida, Key West is one of the most popular to visit by plane – it's at least three hours from Miami. Consider driving in one direction and flying in the other. Not only will it save you time and hassle, it will also provide spectacular views of the Keys. Alternatively, **Cape Air** flies between Naples and Key West. Bookings can be made online (*www.flycapeair.com*).

By bus

Greyhound is the service provider for long-distance bus services in America. In order to make its profit, Greyhound makes many stops along every journey. Coach depots can be found in most major towns and cities in Florida. Bookings can be made online (*www.greyhound.com*).

Bus travel within cities is not recommended as waiting times are often long. Miami's Metrobus system covers almost all of the city.

In the Orlando area, Disney Transportation buses and the Disney Magical Express service offer free transportation throughout the entire Walt Disney World® Resort, as well as to and from Orlando Airport for guests of Disney-owned resort hotels. Many Orlando area hotels and resorts also offer a free shuttle bus service.

By boat

Travelling by water is only an option if you want to visit the Everglades National Park or charter a boat.

Florida is also a very popular cruise terminus, with Fort Lauderdale, Miami and Key West all frequent destinations. Located about 40 minutes from Orlando, Port Canaveral is the home port of **Disney Cruise Lines** (*www.disneycruise.com*).

For those wishing to see Key West, one option to consider is the **Key West Express** high-speed ferry. Tickets cost $135 return and can be booked online (*www.seakeywestexpress.com*).

By taxi

For long trips, taxis are extortionately expensive, so are best avoided. Taxis need to be pre-booked, except in South Beach and Ybor City. The largest taxi service in Orlando is **Mears Transportation Group** (*Tel: (407) 422 2222. www.mears transportation.com/taxiservices.htm*).

Accommodation

Florida offers something to suit everyone's taste and budget. Long dependent on tourists as a source of revenue, the state's hospitality industry is one of the best in the nation, and it has developed to ensure that everyone who wants to visit will. Everyone from antique-buying bed-and-breakfast-goers through to families looking for space and amenities can be catered for (and sometimes right next door to each other).

Historic properties

As home to North America's oldest port, Florida offers many surprises. One of these is the number of historic inns and B&Bs available in resorts throughout the state. While Miami, Tampa, Orlando and the larger towns don't tend to offer much in the way of places of period charm and character, other areas do.

Cavalier Hotel, South Beach

It shouldn't come as much of a shock that St Augustine, North America's first port, offers the widest array of old properties, including Florida's oldest, dating from 1791. Key West is another boutique hotspot with the bulk of accommodation offerings in town coming from converted period cottages.

For antebellum homes and plantation-style inns you'll need to go north to the Panhandle, particularly to the regions surrounding Tallahassee. While there aren't as many Civil War-period properties as in Georgia, Alabama or other Southern states, there are still plenty to give you a taste of staying in the past.

Larger historic resorts are primarily found up and down the Atlantic Coast. Many of these resorts were built by railway tycoon Henry Flagler, who wanted to create stunning destination resorts that would entice chilly Northerners down to Florida's sunny climes and have them use his railway at the same time. At one point, one of his

Vin Mar Motel near Orlando

hotels was the most expensive ever built. His legacy remains in the form of The Breakers, the luxury resort of choice in Palm Beach ever since it was built.

Motels

In Europe and other parts of the United States, motels and motor lodges are less than salubrious places to rest your head, filled as they are with bland furnishings and even blander staff. The popularity (and necessity) of driving in Florida, however, means that the motel is sometimes a must, especially if you are going long distances, and motels in Florida may surprise you. Many are filled with character and great amenities and offer fantastic value in areas that are traditionally seen as high-end. Don't turn your nose up until you check out the interiors for yourself. Be aware that properties on desolate stretches of highway are less likely to offer anything more than the basics.

Hotels and resorts

Florida is all about volume and bigger is often better, especially when it comes to amenities and services. In fact, as of 2009, Florida offered more than 370,000 hotel, motel and resort rooms (with 116,902 of those located in the Orlando area). All of the big international chains, such as Hilton, Marriott, Ramada, Ritz-Carlton, Four Seasons and Sheraton, are well represented throughout Florida, and all provide plenty of options.

When reserving your room, the time of year, view offered, and the room configuration will help determine the nightly or weekly rate. A typical one-room guest room will have two Queen-size beds or one King size; however, to accommodate families, some offer pull-out sofa beds, twin beds or even bunk beds. Many families opt to reserve adjoining rooms or a multi-bedroom suite.

In the Orlando area, staying at one of the Disney resort hotels offers a variety of special perks such as extended hours at the theme parks and free transportation to and from the airport. You'll pay a premium to stay at one of these properties, but their proximity to the theme parks and the added services are worth it to many visitors. You can save money by staying off-property at one of the hundreds of hotels located a short drive from the theme parks.

Townhouse and timeshare rentals

For those in need of more space than that generally offered by an average hotel room, there are two additional options that exist in many parts of Florida. Companies such as All-Star Vacation Homes (see Directory) rent full-size, multi-bedroom townhouses, complete with kitchen, living room, dining room, bathrooms, laundry facilities and other amenities, which are located on resort-like properties close to major cities and attractions. These can be rented by the night or week.

Florida is also where you will find thousands of timeshare holiday properties. Even if you're not a timeshare owner, many of these resorts, including those operated by Marriott Vacation Club (see Directory), offer non-owners the ability to rent spacious multi-bedroom suites by the night or week. These include a living room, kitchen, laundry facilities, a dining area and multiple bathrooms, and they are often located on properties with swimming pools, tennis courts, golf courses, restaurants, organised kids' programmes and other activities. They tend to be near major attractions and cities.

Whether you rent a fully furnished townhouse or a timeshare property, you'll be offered clean, comfortable and roomy accommodation for about the same price as a standard, three-star hotel room for the family. Plus, you can save extra money by preparing your own meals.

Seasons

The peak season for travel in Florida is usually the winter months (except for the north of the state – see p142). From November through to April, prices can as much as double. Over Christmas and Easter, this can increase even more. If you want to save money, either book well in advance or wait until the last minute. If you are a traveller who knows exactly what you are looking for, then advance booking is the way to go in order to ensure availability. Those who book last minute will be able to benefit from scooping up what hasn't sold, although you never know what you will end up with, if anything at all.

Specific regional periods to watch out for, when rooms become impossible to find, include College Spring Break in Panama City, Homecoming Week, Graduation and the Legislative Session in Tallahassee, FantasyFest in Key West, and during space shuttle launches or the Daytona

500 along the Space Coast of Cape Canaveral, Cocoa Beach and Daytona Beach. In Orlando, the peak times are during school holidays and between mid-November and early January. During these times, room rates are higher and vacancies are harder to find.

How to book

It used to be that travellers wanting to visit Florida invariably went straight to a travel agent in order to book their 7- or 14-day package. Times have changed and online travel bookings have done much to revolutionise people's holiday spending patterns. Packagers have woken up to this adjustment and are now offering more alternatives and options than ever before. No longer are you locked into specific durations or obscenely late flight times. Instead, you can now build your own packages while benefiting from the superior knowledge and security an agent can provide. If you are looking to arrange a two-centre break, an agent is often the better option as agencies have the clout to negotiate better rates and can easily organise the transfers between each of your resorts into one simple booking.

For longer stays, driving tours or holidays exploring lesser-known destinations such as the Panhandle and the northern reaches of the Atlantic Coast, online booking may still be the better option as it offers more selection. Be sure that whoever you do book with is bonded and ATOL-licensed before putting any money down on the balance of your holiday.

The Don CeSar Beach Resort in St Pete Beach

Food and drink

All tastes are catered for in Florida, a region that boasts a diverse population cooking up the flavours of the world. Fine dining is often referred to as 'Floribbean', a combination of Caribbean spices with local produce. Expect items on the menu to be fresh (caught that day or grown next door) using Caribbean spices and cooking styles. Families will also appreciate Florida's diverse range of restaurants catering to children's needs. You won't have to look hard for a menu filled with treats your tots will love.

Fast food

Like the rest of the USA, Florida isn't immune to the demand for fast food. Try to avoid the usual burger and pizza suspects in favour of more unusual options to at least experience local fast-food varieties. Ybor City and Little Havana are great places in which to sample a Cuban sandwich, stuffed high with spiced pork or other fillings. Alternatively, Key West offers great fresh-caught fish prepared any way you like to take away.

Drinks and alcohol

The tipple of choice wherever you go is rum. In fact, the international headquarters for the Bacardí family and distillery has been in Florida ever since the Cuban revolution. Most regional cocktails will feature rum of some variety in the concoction.

Beer drinkers will appreciate the fact that Busch Gardens is owned by the family behind Budweiser beer. Inside the grounds is a beer-tasting centre that gives you the chance to try two brews during your stay.

Wine is often drunk with meals at night, but drinking during the day is an activity frowned upon in North America to some extent. It is certainly not as popular a pastime as in Europe. Please note that driving is a must due to the vast distances in Florida. Drinking and driving is a big problem and should be avoided at all costs.

Non-drinkers will love the variety of fresh tropical fruits and juices. Orange juice may have come straight from the tree earlier that day.

Regional specialities

As a state ringed by water, fish and seafood are the best option. Cooking methods vary, but most dishes are prepared simply – lightly broiled with a dash of lemon juice, simple tomato sauces, or sautéed with garlic and olive oil. Deep frying is less popular now but still may be an option in 'country-style' establishments.

Southern cooking

In the Panhandle, where lifestyles are considered more 'Southern' than Floridian, Deep South cuisine is a must. Sample fried chicken like you've never tasted it before, okra, collard greens, green beans with ham hock, po' boys and black-eyed peas. Definitely not for those counting calories or cholesterol!

Vegetarians and allergies

Those who have food allergies or are vegetarian will have no problems. Most menus feature meat-free alternatives and chefs are prepared to adjust cooking methods to cope with allergies.

Themed restaurants

Children and teenagers in particular will enjoy dining at one of the many themed restaurants located throughout Florida (but mostly in Orlando). Some options include the Hard Rock Cafe (Orlando, Hollywood, Miami, Myrtle Beach, Tampa), Planet Hollywood (Orlando, Myrtle Beach) and Rainforest Café (Orlando, Sunrise).

Tipping

Tipping rates are creeping higher every day. Where it was once 15 per cent, it is now getting closer to 20 per cent. The standard rule of thumb should be that, if the service is good, 15 per cent is the minimum to go with. Excellent service should always get 20 per cent.

Food and drink

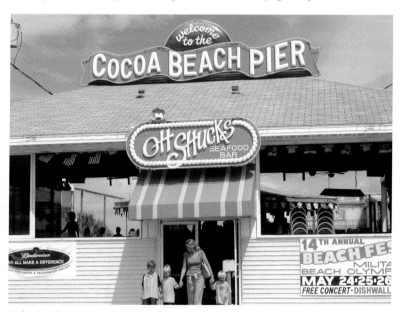

Seafood at the Cocoa Beach Pier

Entertainment

There's something to do almost all of the time in Florida. Dance till dawn with new flamenco steps, listen to Cuban horn in Little Havana or catch a Broadway hit at Coconut Grove. Miami Beach and Ybor City in Tampa are the places to go for a lively party scene. For more sedate and high-brow offerings, stick to Sarasota, Naples and the towns further north along the Atlantic Coast from Miami.

Cafés

Café culture is alive and well in Florida. Thanks to a large Hispanic population that considers a cup of coffee and a chat until the wee hours a must, you can find a good cup of Java anywhere south of Gainesville.

Miami offers the widest range of options, from hip places to see and be seen in South Beach through to Little Havana's Latino nightspots where a cup of coffee can last all night. Tampa's Ybor City also has its fair share of cafés catering to a wide range of tastes.

Restaurants

With such a strong tourism trade, it should come as no surprise that there are plenty of restaurants in Florida, especially in the larger resort towns. Dining out is a regular occurrence and not the luxury that other locations view it as. It's possible to eat at almost every hour of the day somewhere in Florida. So if you're hungry enough, chances are you'll find somewhere to serve you.

Pubs and bars

Drinking establishments in Florida are always popular, with everything from wine bars to biker dens available. Note that the drinking age in Florida is 21 and ID will be needed. Also be aware that drinking and driving is a severe problem in the state. If you have been drinking, do not get behind the wheel of your car.

Cinema

While there are many celebrities who call Florida home, movie-going is less popular an option than in other states. That said, film fans will have their choice of screens in Florida, from major multiplexes with a wide range of screens playing Hollywood blockbusters to converted and restored cinemas from yesteryear specialising in repertory options. Jacksonville and Tampa have two of the finest in America.

Florida is a popular choice for movie-makers as a setting due to the regular sunshine and diversity in the state. Some of the more famous productions to shoot and/or be set in Florida include *True Lies*, *Miami Vice*, *Key Largo*, *Get Shorty*, *There's Something about Mary* and *Scarface*.

Theatre

Live theatre flourishes in Florida. In fact, Florida State University has consistently been rated as one of the top ten theatre schools in the country by *US News and World Report*. Probably the most atmospheric place to see live theatre is at the Asolo Theater in Sarasota, which was transported brick by brick by the circus entrepreneur John Ringling from Italy.

Outside of Asolo, the bulk of theatrical productions can be seen at the various performing arts centres and theatres dotted around the state, such as the Coconut Grove Playhouse or Broward County Center for Performing Arts.

Popular theatrical performance tends to be conservative in Florida in order to cater for the moneyed and mature crowd that patronises it. Broadway transfers in the form of star-studded plays and musicals dominate programming, with the occasional new work thrown in to test boundaries.

For the most adventurous productions, community theatres and college campuses are where you should look, although be advised that quality is very hit and miss. FSU's Tallahassee Campus provides the best chance to see the stars of tomorrow in the productions held at the School of Fine Arts building.

Sloppy Joe's, a favourite haunt of Hemingway's in Key West

Ballet and dance

Dance in Florida is a relatively recent phenomenon but one growing in stature every day. The best known and most highly respected of the lot is the Miami City Ballet located in South Beach. Despite the fact that it was founded less than three decades ago, it is today one of the best-funded and largest ballet companies in America.

For details on dance events across the state, check out the **Florida Dance Association** website (*www.floridadanceassociation.org*).

This is a state-funded organisation that serves to promote dance performance, production and education state-wide.

For something a little more energetic, consider taking in a performance of flamenco or salsa. Florida's large Latino population means that opportunities to see masters at work in these art forms are frequent. You can even pick up a few steps at the regular dance sessions held in clubs and bars in cities with a large Hispanic presence. Have a hunt in Little Havana or Ybor City to see what's what and who's who.

Tower Theater on Calle Ocho in Little Havana

Underwater ballet at Weeki Wachee Springs north of Tampa

Live music

Floridians love their music. Whether it be the hits of native daughter Gloria Estefan and her Miami Sound Machine or the sweet sounds of native son Tom Petty, this state is one where a concert of any form is a highlight.

Miami, with its cosmopolitan population, celebrity residents and easy air access, is the most popular destination for musicians to play in – and play they do. A walk through city streets will reveal reggae, Cuban horn, rap, soul, blues, jazz and everything else you can think of emanating from the local establishments. Live music is often programmed in bars, so even if you can't afford to shell out $100 for that Madonna concert ticket, you can always hear something during your stay.

Classical performances

Despite the fact that Florida has the USA's oldest settlement, it simply isn't a very big player in the world of classical performance. Never fear if the sound of a symphony appeals, however; during the summer you can often find the London Symphony Orchestra performing in Daytona Beach, the unofficial second home of the group. They have played in Daytona more often than anywhere else on the planet!

Two organisations to look out for are the New World Symphony of Miami Beach and the Jacksonville Symphony, known nationwide for their new works. Don't go if modern classical music is not to your liking.

Shopping

For many international travellers a trip to the United States has nothing to do with culture or sun-worshipping and everything to do with the amount of damage they can do to their wallet. Exchange rates are extremely advantageous to international travellers, making a trip to the mall a true bargain. While local specialities are few, there are still enough regional items to spark memories back home. T-shirts are the cheapest option, but key lime candles, cigars from Ybor and artworks are all native to the state.

Souvenirs

You can pretty much find whatever you could possibly want sold as a memento of your visit. As the battle for the tourist dollar is so intense, be sure to shop around before making souvenir purchases as '2 for 1' and other discounts are common enough. If you see something unique, then pick it up by all means. Just be aware that many shops in a single community sell the same things so it's good to comparison shop if you have the time.

Within the various Disney theme parks you will find the best selection of authentic Disney souvenirs and merchandise. The world's largest Disney Store is located within Downtown Disney®. The Universal Orlando, SeaWorld® and Busch Gardens theme parks also offer many gift shops and souvenir kiosks.

Shopping malls

Climate-controlled shopping centres are the way to go in Florida and there are certainly plenty to go to. While the typical visitor may wonder about the appeal of going inside when visiting the Sunshine State, they'll certainly appreciate it on days when humidity hits 100 per cent and the temperature is soaring.

Going to the mall for the average American isn't just a chance to shop – it's a social occasion. Here is where teens congregate, the elderly stroll and families meet up to chat and go to the cinema. Mega-malls in Florida make most European versions look small, with the typical set-up having a food court of fast-food outlets in the centre, at least 100 or more retail outlets and a couple of lead department stores acting as 'anchors' at either end. There may also be an entertainment complex attached offering a multi-screen cinema. It's a great place to kill time when you're too hot or the storms arrive and you need to keep out of the wet.

High-end shopping in Worth Avenue, Palm Beach

Ethnic options

With such a diverse population, it should come as no surprise that ethnic shopping is huge. For a slice of Latin culture, including Santería religious products or Caribbean foodstuffs, Miami's Little Havana is the place to go. Ybor City in Tampa also has a history as a cigar-making and distribution point, so deals on stogies are a true find. You can even see locals rolling them in front of your very eyes.

Outlets and discounts

Say the word 'outlet' to a shopper and you may find their eyes glowing in anticipation and glee. An outlet specialises in selling out-of-season, sample and discontinued stock by leading designers at greatly reduced prices. Florida is the outlet capital of the country, with stores and even entire malls dedicated to outlet shopping scattered throughout the state. By far the most famous of the bunch is Sawgrass Mills in Fort Lauderdale, a massive collection of over 350 discounted retailers including Gap and Saks Fifth Avenue.

When purchasing at outlets, be sure to check that the quality of the item is good. There's a reason why these items were sent here, so look for snags or tears in the fabric. Also, keep your head together and think twice as to whether you really need that fluorescent pink T-shirt with the diamante trim. It may have walked down the catwalk in 2001, but will it really hold up to critical gazes today?

Designer goods

As Florida has a strong economy, the opportunities to find designer merchandise are rife. Palm Beach's Worth Avenue has prime designer pickings, with boutiques such as Chanel and Hermès boasting places on its pricey real estate. While in Miami, Bal Harbour is the best area for shopping, especially the shopping centre known as Bal Harbour Shops. In Tampa, International Plaza, with its branches of Neiman Marcus and Saks Fifth Avenue, is the place to head for.

Outside of these three main areas, designer goods may be more limited.

Instead, you'll find smaller-scale boutiques catering to a small circle of elite: politicians and their wives in Tallahassee, old-money residents, and retirees in Naples. You may not have such a wide range, but the items will be unique.

Consumer goods and electronics

Compared to Europe, prices on consumer goods such as iPods and laptop computers are very good. In fact, due to the lower combined sales tax, purchasing items in Florida rather than New York City can save you money. However, be aware that many gaming

St Armand's Circle, Sarasota

Shopping in the historic centre of Fernandina Beach

systems will only play games purchased in America, so if you have plans to buy a PS3, you won't be able to purchase any games for your system in the UK.

Sales tax

Sales tax in Florida is set at 6 per cent, but some cities and counties add an extra percentage depending on where you are. Restaurant and hotel bills are sometimes liable to additional surcharges, so be sure to check on the menu or hotel website before making your selections as you could be surprised by a supplement of as much as 10 per cent on top.

Customs and duty

As more and more travellers are choosing to make their wardrobe purchases abroad, customs officers are wising up. Check permitted purchase levels in advance so that you aren't stung with a massive duty payment when you return home. Returning to your home nation after just three days away with three full suitcases is a huge giveaway that you may not have been spending all of your time on the beach. Trying to sneak your items past a customs officer's critical gaze will merely serve to add insult to financial injury.

Sport and leisure

Floridians are active souls. One look at the bronzed and toned bodies on South Beach should be enough to convince you of this fact. Depending on where you are visiting, each area has its speciality, so while kayaking may be the thing to do in one town, the next might prefer to do their workouts in a gym or health centre. And with almost permanent sunshine, you'll have no excuse not to keep your body healthy and happy.

Diving and snorkelling

As a state surrounded by water, diving opportunities are rife. Florida doesn't boast the same volume of reefs that other holiday destinations such as the Maldives and Australia offer, but that doesn't mean there isn't much to see. The Keys are the place to go for those who are looking to explore life underwater. In fact, you can even live underwater at an intriguing hotel built on the ocean floor in Key Largo! Dive centres are competitively priced and all are licensed, meaning that you can guarantee that equipment is kept in good working order. To find a centre right for you, it is worth shopping around before making any commitments. Price may be one guide, but trust in your instructor and word of mouth should be taken into account just as much.

Golf

Florida has a huge number of championship golf courses. Depending on your price range, you can choose to tee off at reasonably priced municipal courses, hotel-based greens or private clubs. Obviously, the more expensive and elite the course, the less competition there will be for good tee times. Don't be dismayed if you can't snag a membership or afford entry to a private course, however, as municipal courses are very well maintained – you just might have to begin your session on the links a little earlier or later than you might like. Be sure to book your times at least two or three days in advance, or more if you can manage it. Florida is also a great place to pick up a set of clubs, with prices often far less than you would pay back home. Rentals are available at most pro shops and golf centres.

Hiking and biking

Trails abound in Florida, with islands offering incredible short journeys for those who are just looking for a day trip, specifically Sanibel Island and Key

Biscayne. For longer trips, head to the Panhandle where Apalachicola National Forest offers abundant opportunities to get back to nature. The 30-mile (48km) trail that runs through the forest will challenge even the most dedicated rambler, but the opportunity to see some of Florida's flora and fauna will more than make up for the sweat and bother. Bike rentals can be done near the areas you are hoping to explore. (*See pp136–41.*)

Kayaking and canoeing

The Florida Keys, Everglades and southwest coast are great kayak and canoe hotspots due to the varied topography. Island-hopping along the Keys is a great way to spend the day just as much as an exploration of the mangrove forests and swamps of the Corkscrew Swamp Sanctuary. Canoe rental prices are competitive, but a day trip in the swamp in high humidity is not advised. When in doubt, join a guided tour where you

Kayaking on the Estero River

Sailing is a great way to see Florida's coastline

will have the added backup of a qualified guide who can get you out of sticky situations.

Sailing

Chartering a yacht or boat is easy to do, with almost every major resort offering competitive prices. Fort Lauderdale, Naples and Key West offer the widest selection and most interesting itineraries. Once again, it is best to shop around before making any commitment, as price should not be the only thing you base your selection on; ship maintenance and trust in the captain or crew should be just as important when booking your day trip or extended sail.

Spas and relaxation

Sauna and massage facilities are considered a must for any high-end resort. Amelia Island, Palm Beach, Miami and Naples all boast some of America's leading facilities. While spas at these properties are open to the public, you might find prices a little on the high side. Public facilities are less common. You won't find public baths, hammams or thermal baths anywhere in the state. This kind of activity is reserved for those who have the money to pay for it (and if you do have the cash, it's well worth the investment). Less a spa and more a tropical swimming pool is the Venetian Pool in Coral Gables (*see p34*). There aren't any massage facilities at this swimming pool, but the lush greenery and coral rock surrounding it will make you feel like you're in paradise.

Surfing

Riding the waves isn't as popular in Florida as in Hawaii or California, but Cocoa Beach does have a vibrant surfing community that is worth checking out. Holidaymakers can learn to dive at one of the local schools, which are good for novice surfers, or simply hang with the surfing crowd at the world-famous Ron Jon Surf Shop, a great place to pick up a souvenir.

Working out

Gyms are prevalent throughout the state, with many centres offering day passes to those on a temporary visit. Almost every hotel of three-star calibre or above will have an on-site fitness centre of sorts, so if keeping trim is a priority, it's worth looking at facilities online before making your booking. While gym membership is popular state-wide, South Beach is where working out truly becomes a religion of sorts. Less a pastime and more a dating ritual, the gyms of South Beach are the places to see and be seen. Leading national chain Crunch is the first port of call for many, offering a diverse range of classes, including the Drag Queen workout for ladies who need help toning in order to get through a day on towering Jimmy Choos, or the firefighter workout led by actual firemen and firewomen from the area.

The famous Ron Jon Surf Shop in Cocoa Beach

Children

Children love Florida and Florida loves children. With the many theme parks and family-friendly attractions in Orlando, for example, this state is America's playground and was tailor-made for those who want to bring tots, 'tweens' and teens along on the journey. Prices are inflated during school holiday periods when demand is high, but deals can still be had depending on where you go. Keep a lookout for 'kids stay free' or 'kids eat free' deals in order to keep costs down.

Amusement parks

Busch Gardens in Tampa is the place to go for those who love thrill rides. If your stay takes you to the Panhandle, Panama City Beach with its **Shipwreck Island Water Park** also has water-based rides to enjoy, albeit on a smaller scale.

Busch Gardens. 3000 E Busch Boulevard, Tampa. Tel: (888) 800 5447.
www.buschgardens.com.
Open: 10am–6pm. Admission charge.
Shipwreck Island Water Park. 12201 Middle Beach Road, Panama City Beach. Tel: (850) 234 3333.
www.shipwreckisland.com.
Open: Jun–Jul daily 10.30am–5.30pm; Apr–May & Aug–Sept, times vary – call for details. Admission charge.

Museums

One attraction to highlight is the new **Children's Museum of Naples** set to open in 2010.

North Naples Regional Park, 15000 Livingston Road. Tel: (239) 514 0084.
www.cmon.org. Open: see website for up-to-date information.
Admission charge.

Science centres

Learn about the wonders of nature, chemistry, geology and more by setting the kids free in **G Wiz** in Sarasota, St Petersburg's **Great Explorations** or **MOSI** in Tampa.

G Wiz (Gulfcoast Wonder and Imagination Zone). 1001 Boulevard of the Arts, Sarasota. Tel: (941) 906 1851.
www.gwiz.org. Open: Tue–Sat 10am–5pm, Sun noon–5pm.
Admission charge.
Great Explorations. 1925 4th Avenue N, St Petersburg. Tel: (727) 821 8992.
www.greatexplorations.org.
Open: Mon–Sat 10am–8pm, Sun 11am–5pm. Admission charge.
MOSI (Museum of Science and Industry). 4801 E Fowler Avenue, Tampa. Tel: (813) 987 6100.
www.mosi.org. Open: 9am–5pm.
Admission charge.

Space: The Final Frontier

Head over to the **Kennedy Space Center** if your kids look to the skies. Here you can witness space shuttle launches or visit the visitor information centre and take a tour of the Cape Canaveral site.

Kennedy Space Center. NASA Parkway, Cape Canaveral. Tel: (321) 449 4444. www.kennedyspacecenter.com. Open: 9am–5.30pm. Admission charge.

Zoos and aquariums

Florida boasts an incredible array of animal life. Find out more about Florida's animal wonders by visiting the **Clearwater Marine Aquarium**, **Jacksonville Zoo** or the **Lion Country Safari** in Palm Beach where animals are encouraged to roam the grounds.

Clearwater Marine Aquarium. 249 Windward Passage, Clearwater. Tel: (727) 441 1790. www.cmaquarium.org. Open: Mon–Fri 9am–5pm, Sat 9am–4pm, Sun 11am–4pm. Admission charge.

Jacksonville Zoo and Gardens. 8605 Zoo Parkway, Jacksonville. Tel: (904) 757 4462. www.jaxzoo.org. Open: 9am–5pm. Admission charge.

Lion Country Safari. 2003 Lion Country Safari Road, Loxahatchee. Tel: (561) 793 1084. www.lioncountrysafari.com. Open: 9.30am–5.30pm. Admission charge.

Meet an astronaut at the Kennedy Space Center

Essentials

Arriving and departing
By air
The two airports with the most international connections are located in Miami and Tampa.

Miami International Airport *Tel: (305) 876 7000. www.miami-airport.com*
Tampa International Airport *Tel: (813) 870 8770. www.tampaairport.com*

American Airlines *Tel: 0845 7789 789. www.americanairlines.co.uk*
British Airways *Tel: 0870 850 9850. www.ba.com*
Virgin Atlantic *Tel: 0870 380 2007. www.virgin-atlantic.com*

By sea
Dozens of cruise lines operate routes in and out of Florida's cruise terminals. Most, however, cannot be used to reach Florida as a destination. There are occasional turnaround cruises that bring liners from the Med routes to Florida in time for the Caribbean winter season.

Cruise ship docked in Miami

By train
Three routes travel through Florida: two along the Atlantic and one stretching across the country from Los Angeles to Orlando.
Amtrak *Tel: reservations (UK) 001 800 872 7245. www.amtrak.com*

By car
There are three main roads leading into Florida from other parts of the United States. The two most commonly used highways are I-75 and I-95 from Georgia. Both are popular routes; however, I-75 is better used for Orlando and Tampa, while I-95 is the route to take to Jacksonville, Cape Canaveral, Miami and the Atlantic Coast resorts. From Alabama, Mississippi and Louisiana, I-10 through Pensacola, Tallahassee and Jacksonville is the road to take. The I-10 connects with I-75 and I-95 if you plan to drive south.

Customs
Most personal effects and the following items are duty-free: 200 cigarettes or 50 cigars (not Cuban) or 2kg of smoking tobacco, one litre of wines or spirits (if you're over 21), up to $100 in gifts, and

$10,000 in cash, traveller's cheques or endorsed bank drafts.

Electricity

The standard electrical current is 110–120V. Plugs have two flat pins; adaptors can be purchased at most electrical shops.

Internet

Internet access is prevalent across the state at reasonable costs. In-room Wi-Fi is standard in many hotels at a premium. Many towns also now offer Wi-Fi hotspots. Thanks to international roaming, mobile phones and other devices will have no trouble connecting to the wireless web throughout Florida.

Money

The currency in the United States is the dollar. A dollar is divided into 100 cents. You can withdraw money using ATMs at almost all American banks. Credit cards are widely accepted for almost all transactions, with Visa, MasterCard and American Express the most common forms of plastic. Try to use an ATM whenever possible as it will always give you the bank rate for the day. If that's not possible, American banks are your next best alternative. Bureaux de change are less common in American cities, especially outside main centres like Miami and Tampa.

Opening hours

Most businesses open Mon–Fri 10am–6pm. Shopping centres always stay open later, until about 9pm. Cultural institutions are usually open 9am–6pm, although selected days during the week often have extended opening hours.

Passports and visas

Visitors to the United States who are citizens of countries under the Visa Waiver Scheme such as the UK, Ireland, Australia and New Zealand will need a machine-readable passport, but not a visa, for stays of 90 days or less. Canadians do not need visas but will need a valid passport. South African citizens do require a visa.

Pharmacies

Many pharmacy chains, such as Walgreens, CVS and Rite Aid, have locations throughout Florida that are open 24 hours a day. In addition to being able to refill prescriptions, you will find a vast assortment of over-the-counter medications and other necessities (sun block, snacks and toiletries). Medication that can be bought over the counter in your home may require a prescription in Florida.

Post

Stamps can be bought at post offices or from most drugstores. Post boxes are blue. Postcards to destinations within the USA cost 23¢, and to Europe 70¢.

Public holidays

New Year's Day 1 Jan
Martin Luther King Jr Day 3rd Mon in Jan
Presidents' Day 3rd Mon in Feb
Memorial Day last Mon in May
Independence Day 4 July
Labor Day 1st Mon in Sept
Columbus Day 2nd Mon in Oct
Veterans' Day 11 Nov
Thanksgiving Day 4th Thur in Nov
Christmas Day 25 Dec

Smoking

In most cities and regions of Florida, smoking has been completely banned in all public buildings, including restaurants and bars. However, in Miami, Jacksonville and Tampa, smoking in some public buildings is still permitted.

Suggested reading and media

The Miami Herald Miami's major daily and a good resource for everything going on in the city. Daily hurricane updates are available in both the print and online versions.
Ernest Hemingway The noted novelist wrote *To Have and Have Not* during his years living in Key West.
Carl Hiaasen Satirical crime novels are the speciality of this writer, most famous for his work *Striptease*, which was later made into a film.

Elmore Leonard Former journalist Elmore Leonard has written many novels set in south Florida. Pick up a copy of *Get Shorty* to get a flavour of what to expect.

Sustainable tourism

Thomas Cook is a strong advocate of ethical and fairly traded tourism and believes that the travel experience should be as good for the places visited as it is for the people that visit them. That's why we're a firm supporter of The Travel Foundation: a charity that develops solutions to help improve and protect holiday destinations, their environment, traditions and culture. To find out what you can do to make a positive difference to the places you travel to and the people who live there, please visit *www.thetravelfoundation.org.uk*

Tax

State sales tax is set at 6 per cent and is applicable to everything you buy. Some counties also have an extra sales tax of about 1 per cent. Additional taxes are imposed on accommodation and rental cars.

Telephones

Telephoning from Florida

When making an international call from the United States, dial the international code you require (*see below*), then the area code, dropping the initial zero, followed by the local number.

The international codes for calls from the USA are as follows:

Australia *01161*
New Zealand *01164*
Republic of Ireland *011353*
South Africa *01127*
UK *01144*

Calls to Canada do not require an international dialling code.

Telephoning Florida

In order to call Florida from abroad, you will need to know the seven-digit number plus the three-digit area code prefix specific to the city you are calling. As an example, if the number you are calling is *(954) 555 1212*, then you will need to ring the international dialling code + *1 + 954 + 555 1212*.

Mobiles

In some more remote areas, you may find poor signals, but the signal will be strong in all major cities and around popular tourist attractions.

While you will be able to use your mobile in the USA, international roaming charges will probably be high. A more affordable alternative is to purchase a US-based prepaid phone or a local SIM card for your unlocked GSM phone, both of which are readily available from convenience stores and mobile phone shops. The least expensive way to call overseas, however, is to use a prepaid calling card or a Voice-Over-IP service from a computer that is connected to the Internet (using Skype, for example).

Time

Clocks in Florida follow Eastern Standard Time (EST). During Daylight Saving Time (end Mar–end Oct), the clocks are put ahead one hour. In Miami at noon, the time at home is as follows:

Australia Eastern Standard Time 3am (next day), Central Standard Time 2.30am (next day), Western Standard Time 2am (next day)
New Zealand 6am (next day)
South Africa 7pm
UK and Republic of Ireland 5pm
USA and Canada Newfoundland Time 1.30pm, Atlantic Canada Time 1pm, Central Time 11am, Mountain Time 10am, Pacific Time 9am, Alaska 8am

Toilets

Locals make use of the public facilities at the numerous shopping centres that are scattered throughout the state. Restaurants, bars and hotels generally don't have too much of a problem if you use their restrooms. Also, petrol stations may have facilities.

Travellers with disabilities

Facilities for visitors with disabilities are generally quite good in the United States. A useful source of advice when in Florida is the **Society for the Advancement of Travel for the Handicapped** (*Tel: (212) 447 7284. www.sath.org*).

Emergencies

Emergency numbers

Ambulance, Fire brigade, Police *911*

Medical services
Casualty

If you have a medical emergency, call *911* to reach ambulance services to take you to the casualty (known as the emergency) wing of your nearest hospital. If possible, try to bring a copy of your travel insurance policy with you as some establishments will not offer treatment unless you can show proof that you are covered. American medical services are among the best in the world, but you will have to pay for the privilege of using the facilities.

For less serious injuries, 24-hour pharmacies can be found in most major cities. Ask your hotel for the closest one available.

Doctors

There is a doctor specialising in almost everything in Florida, especially in the main centres. Specialists can be seen almost immediately if you have travel insurance. All are English-speaking, so you should have no trouble explaining what ails you.

Ocean rescue vehicle in Fort Lauderdale

Opticians

Unlike in the UK, opticians tend not to work from spectacle shops. Instead, you will need to make an appointment at their clinic. Check with the concierge of your hotel for recommendations. Prescription glasses can usually be turned around within 24 hours.

Health and travel insurance

Comprehensive travel insurance is a must whenever you travel to the United States due to the massive health costs you will incur should you require treatment or hospitalisation. You'll need health insurance for treatment with most medical professionals. If you do not purchase it before you go away, you'll have to provide a credit card upon admittance to a hospital. But medical costs are so high that you would be likely to exceed your credit limit very quickly.

Health risks

It is not necessary to take any special health precautions while travelling in Florida. Tap water is safe to drink, although many locals prefer to drink bottled varieties.

Police

Should you require police assistance, dial 911 and the appropriate police branch (State, City or Highway Patrol) will come to your rescue. Police officers are ubiquitous in highly touristed locations, and have been ever since

Miami's crime wave of the 1980s and 1990s affected inbound tourism numbers across the state.

Safety and crime

As in any other high-density destination, crime is a fact of life. Most cases of violent crime are restricted to neighbourhoods you will be unlikely to visit during your stay. One exception is Downtown Miami, which is fine during the daylight hours in the week, but can become decidedly unwelcoming after dark and on weekends. Gentrification has already started in this neighbourhood, so the situation could change shortly. Other tricky areas include Ybor City in Tampa and Frenchtown in Tallahassee.

Embassies and consulates

Australian Embassy *1601 Massachusetts Avenue NW, Washington DC. Tel: (202) 797 3000. www.usa.embassy.gov.au*
Canadian Consulate *Suite 1600, 200 S Biscayne Boulevard, Miami. Tel: (305) 579 1600. www.dfait-maeci.gc.ca*
Irish Embassy *2234 Massachusetts Avenue NW, Washington DC. Tel: (202) 462 3939. www.irelandemb.org*
New Zealand Embassy *37 Observatory Circle NW, Washington DC. Tel: (202) 328 4800. www.nzembassy.com*
UK Consulate *Suite 2800, 1001 S Brickell Bay Drive, Miami. Tel: (305) 374 1522. www.britainusa.com*

Directory

Accommodation price guide

All price ranges given are for a double room exclusive of taxes.

★	Under $100
★★	$100–200
★★★	$200–300
★★★★	Over $300

Eating out price guide

All price ranges given are for a single course per person, without drinks.

★	Under $7
★★	$7–12
★★★	$12–18
★★★★	Over $18

MIAMI AND THE SOUTH ATLANTIC COAST

Downtown Miami

ACCOMMODATION

Miami River Inn ★
Historic bed and breakfast located close to the Downtown core. Both the exterior, which dates from 1906, and the interior have a New England feel.
118 SW South River Drive at SW 4th Avenue.
Tel: (305) 325 0045.
www.miamiriverinn.com

Mandarin Oriental Miami ★★★
Miami's branch of the luxury chain.
500 Brickell Key Drive at Brickell Avenue.
Tel: (305) 913 8288.
www.mandarin-oriental.com/miami

EATING OUT

People's Bar-B-Que ★★
Delicious home cooking at a soul shack. This is barbecue done right – served up with black-eyed peas, collard greens and smothered in sauce.
360 NW 8th Street at NW 3rd Avenue.
Tel: (305) 373 8080.
Open: Mon–Thur 11.30am–11.30pm, Fri & Sat 11.30am–1am, Sun 1–9pm.

Joe's Seafood ★★★
Great Latin-spiced seafood within a relaxed eatery boasting incredible views over the Miami River.
400 NW North River Drive at NW 4th Street.
Tel: (305) 374 5637.
Open: Mon–Thur & Sun 11am–10pm, Fri & Sat 11am–11pm.

ENTERTAINMENT

Adrienne Arsht Center
Designed by architect César Pelli, this jewel in the crown of Miami's artistic scene is home to Broadway musical transfers, visiting world-renowned musicians, ballet, opera, lecture series... you name it.
1300 Biscayne Boulevard between 13th and 14th Streets.
Tel: (305) 949 6722.
www.miamipac.org

SPORT AND LEISURE

Miami Heat (Basketball)
See Miami's smokin' basketball team, the Miami Heat, in action at the American Airlines

Arena downtown.
*601 Biscayne Boulevard
at NE 6th Street.
Tel: (786) 777 1000.
www.nba.com/heat*

Coconut Grove
ACCOMMODATION
**Grove Isle Hotel and
Spa ★★★**
Beautiful bay views and
lush gardens meet Miami
colour and splash.
*Grove Isle Drive off
S Bayshore Drive.
Tel: (305) 858 8300.
www.groveisle.com*

EATING OUT
Scotty's Landing ★
Cheap and cheerful beer
and seafood shack. Good
food at great prices.
*3381 Pan American Drive
at S Bayshore Drive.
Tel: (305) 854 2626.
Open: Mon–Thur 11am–
10pm, Fri–Sun 11am–
11pm.*
**Le Bouchon du
Grove ★★★★**
Fine French dining with
excellent service.
*3430 Main Highway at
Grand Avenue.
Tel: (305) 448 6060.
Open: Mon–Thur 10am–
3pm & 5–11pm, Fri
10am–3pm & 5pm–*

*midnight, Sat 8am–3pm
& 5pm–midnight, Sun
8am–3pm & 5–11pm.*

SPORT AND LEISURE
Crook & Crook (Fishing)
For tackle, information
and tips on which
charter operators to go
with, head down to
Crook & Crook.
*2795 SW 27th Avenue at
US 1. Tel: (305) 854 0005.
www.crookandcrook.com.
Open: Mon–Fri 7am–
8pm, Sat 6am–8pm,
Sun 6am–3pm.*

Coral Gables
ACCOMMODATION
**Best Western
ChateauBleau Hotel ★**
Good-value property
with basic furnishings.
*1111 Ponce de Leon
Boulevard at Antilla
Avenue.
Tel: (305) 448 2634. www.
hotelchateaubleau.com*
Biltmore ★★★
An icon of Coral Gables
and the hotel that
established the
neighbourhood as
the place to see and be
seen when it was built
in 1925.
*1200 Anastasia Avenue
at Granada Boulevard.*

*Tel: (305) 445 1926.
www.biltmorehotel.com*

ENTERTAINMENT
GableStage
The best theatre in town
for Broadway and
London hits.
*Biltmore Hotel, 1200
Anastasia Avenue at
Granada Boulevard.
Tel: (305) 445 1119.
www.gablestage.org*

SPORT AND LEISURE
Biltmore Hotel (Golf)
Originally designed and
built in 1925, the
Biltmore Hotel's
championship 18-hole
golf course is still a
favourite.
*1210 Anastasia Avenue at
Granada Boulevard.
Tel: (305) 445 8066.
www.biltmorehotel.com.
Open: 7am–6.30pm.*
**Salvadore Park
Tennis Center**
Great weather and a
plethora of courts
make this spot popular
with locals.
*1120 Andalusia Avenue at
Columbus Boulevard.
Tel: (305) 460 5333.
Open: Mon–Fri 7am–
9pm, Sat & Sun
7am–8pm.*

South Beach
ACCOMMODATION
Century ★
An affordable find with Art Deco furnishings.
140 Ocean Drive at 1st Street.
Tel: (305) 674 8855. www.centurysouthbeach.com

Park Central ★★
Art Deco meets the present day in this wonderful hotel that features a rooftop sundeck.
640 Ocean Drive at 6th Street.
Tel: (305) 538 1611.
www.theparkcentral.com

EATING OUT
News Café ★★
Open 24 hours, News Café offers the best people-watching in town.
800 Ocean Drive at 8th Street.
Tel: (305) 538 6397.
www.newscafe.com

Blue Door ★★★★
Can't afford to stay at the Delano? Do the next best thing and eat at this restaurant that is a delight for both the eye and the stomach.
Delano Hotel, 1685 Collins Avenue at 17th Street.
Tel: (305) 672 2000.
www.delano-hotel.com.
Open: Mon–Thur & Sun 11.30am–4pm & 7pm–midnight, Fri & Sat 11.30am–4pm & 7pm–1am.

ENTERTAINMENT
Club Nikki
Amazing beach club filled with the taut and toned.
1 Ocean Drive at 1st Street.
Tel: (305) 538 1111. www.nikkibeach.com/miami.
Open: Sat & Sun 11pm–5am.

Miami City Ballet
Founded over two decades ago, Miami City Ballet is today one of America's largest.
2200 Liberty Avenue at 22nd Street.
Tel: (305) 929 7000.
www.miamicityballet.org

SPORT AND LEISURE
Crunch Fitness (Gym)
This hotspot health club in South Beach is known for its diverse range of classes.
1259 Washington Avenue at 12th Street.
Tel: (305) 674 8222.
www.crunch.com.
Open: Mon–Fri 6am–midnight, Sat 8am–8pm, Sun 9am–8pm.

South Beach (Swimming)
Miami Beach Patrol Ocean Rescue, 1001 Ocean Drive.
Tel: (305) 673 7714.

Little Havana
EATING OUT
Versailles ★★
The culinary heart of Little Havana. Widely held to be the best for authenticity, atmosphere and sheer buzz.
3555 Calle Ocho at SW 35th Avenue.
Tel: (305) 444 0240.
Open: Mon–Thur 8am–2.30am, Fri 8am–3.30am, Sat 8am–4.30am, Sun 9am–1am.

ENTERTAINMENT
Café Panza
Flamenco show and dance lessons held every Tuesday and Thursday in the heart of Little Havana.
1620 SW 8th Street at SW 16th Avenue.
Tel: (305) 643 5343.
Open: Tue–Sat 11am–2am.

SPORT AND LEISURE
**Orange Bowl
(American football)**
The University of
Miami's beloved
Hurricanes football team
plays in the Orange Bowl
to massive crowds and
great fan support.
*Orange Bowl, 1501 NW 3rd
Street at NW 14th Avenue.
Tel: (305) 643 7100.
www.hurricanesports.com*

Fort Lauderdale
ACCOMMODATION
Pillars ★★
This well-situated hotel
has great service and
elegant interiors.
*111 N Birch Road.
Tel: (954) 467 9639.
www.pillarshotel.com*

EATING OUT
**Blue Moon Fish
Company ★★★★**
Fantastic fish and
seafood make this
restaurant stand out
from the crowd.
*4403 W Tradewinds
Avenue. Tel: (954)
267 9888. www.
bluemoonfishco.com.
Open: Mon–Thur & Sun
11.30am–3pm & 6–10pm,
Fri & Sat 11.30am–3pm
& 6–11pm.*

ENTERTAINMENT
Karma Lounge
Progressive house club
for a glamorous clientele.
*4 W Las Olas Boulevard.
Tel: (954) 523 7159.
Open: Wed & Thur
10pm–3am, Fri & Sat
10pm–4am.*

SPORT AND LEISURE
Aloha Watersports
Rent jet-skis, catamarans
and pleasure craft or
sign up for surfing
lessons at Aloha
Watersports.
*Marriott's Harbor Beach
Resort, 3030 Holiday Drive.
Tel: (954) 462 7245.
www.alohawatersports.com*

Boca Raton
ACCOMMODATION
**Boca Raton Resort and
Club ★★**
The most expensive hotel
ever built upon its
completion in 1926. The
glory has faded a little but
the charm and wealth of
amenities remain.
*501 E Camino Real.
Tel: (888) 543 1277.
www.bocaresort.com*

ENTERTAINMENT
Florida Symphonic Pops
Hear popular favourites
such as movie
soundtracks and
jazz performed by
this professional
orchestra. Call for
performance times,
schedules and locations.
Tel: (561) 393 7677.

SPORT AND LEISURE
**Boca Raton Municipal
Golf Course**
This course offers
18 holes of affordable
golf. Book ahead.
*8111 Golf Course Road.
Tel: (561) 483 6100.*

**Palm Beach and West
Palm Beach**
ACCOMMODATION
The Breakers ★★★
Built by Flagler,
The Breakers remains
the address of choice
in Palm Beach.
*1 South County Road.
Tel: (561) 655 6611.
www.thebreakers.com*

EATING OUT
Rhythm Café ★★★
Menus change daily
at this restaurant that
puts the focus on the
flavour more than the
interiors. Fish dishes are
the speciality of the
house.

3800 S Dixie Highway.
Tel: (561) 833 3406.
Open: Tue–Sat 6–10pm,
Sun 5.30–9pm (Dec–Mar
only).

ENTERTAINMENT

Dr Feel Good's
Bar & Grill

Large, Caribbean-themed
nightclub with regular
theme nights.
219 Clematis Street.
Tel: (561) 833 6500.
www.drfeelgoodsbar.com.
Open: Thur–Sat
9am–3am.

SPORT AND LEISURE

West Palm Beach
Fishing Club

Get all the information
you need about local
fishing options from here.
Tel: (561) 832 6780.

Jupiter and Jupiter Island

ACCOMMODATION

Jupiter Beach
Resort ★★★

The only resort in
Jupiter right on the
beach. Great deals
available in the off-
season.
5 N A1A.
Tel: (561) 746 2511. www.
jupiterbeachresort.com

EATING OUT

The Bistro ★★

Home-style restaurant
offering simple yet
delicious seafood and
continental favourites.
2133 US 1.
Tel: (561) 744 5054.
www.thebistrojupiter.com.
Open: Sun–Thur 5–10pm,
Fri & Sat 4–11pm.

SPORT AND LEISURE

Jupiter's Roger Dean
Stadium (Baseball)

See the St Louis
Cardinals play here
during spring training or
catch minor-league
teams competing the rest
of the year.
4751 Main Street.
Tel: (561) 775 1818).

THE FLORIDA KEYS
Key Largo

ACCOMMODATION

John Pennekamp Coral
Reef State Park ★

Well-maintained
camping ground located
in one of the Upper Keys'
finest parks. Pitches are
tiny in size but well
equipped with showers
and toilets. Tanners and
divers will appreciate the
great beaches and scuba
options.

US 1 at Mile Marker 102.5.
Tel: (305) 451 1202.
www.pennekamppark.com

Kona Kai Resort &
Gallery ★★★

Adults-only resort and
art gallery filled with
refined furnishings
and simple touches
like hammocks and
plentiful chaise longues.
Activities such as
kayaking and tennis
lessons are free of charge
for guests.
97802 Overseas Highway.
Tel: (305) 852 7200.
www.konakairesort.com

Jules' Undersea
Lodge ★★★★

Located 21ft (6.5m)
underwater, this two-
room suite was originally
built as a research centre.
Guests reach the room by
diving to the ocean floor
and then popping up
through a pool in the
suite floor.
51 Shoreland Drive.
Tel: (305) 451 2353.
www.jul.com

EATING OUT

Calypso's Seafood
Grill ★★

Unpretentious eatery for
those in search of a
casual place to enjoy

great seafood. Service can
be a little slow.
1 Seagate Boulevard.
Tel: (305) 451 0600.
Open: Mon–Thur & Sun
11.30am–10pm, Fri & Sat
11.30am–11pm.

SPORT AND LEISURE
**John Pennekamp Coral
Reef State Park (Diving)**
This park offers
incredible diving as
part of the only living
coral reef in the
continental United
States. There is also an
artificial wreck 6 miles
(10km) off the coast, a
former US Navy Landing
Ship Dock.
US 1 at Mile Marker 102.5.
Tel: (305) 451 1202.
www.pennekamppark.com

Along US 1
ACCOMMODATION
Ragged Edge Resort ★
Affordable Polynesian-
style resort with limited
facilities. Great for
families thanks to the
on-site heated pool and
in-room kitchens.
243 Treasure Harbor
Road at Mile Marker
86.5, Islamorada.
Tel: (305) 852 5389.
www.ragged-edge.com

Parmer's Resort ★★
Various cottages with
simple furnishings –
some have kitchens,
others boast oceanside
settings. Repeat bookers
regularly pack the place
out, drawn to the
property's combination
of great service and
affordability.
565 Barry Avenue at Mile
Marker 28.5,
Little Torch Key.
Tel: (305) 872 2157.
www.parmersresort.com

Casa Morada ★★★
A chic, design-focused
boutique resort with only
16 suites. The service is
top-notch. The clientele
tend to be younger and
hipper than at other Key
properties, which is great
for creative types and
those who want a
younger vibe.
136 Madeira Road,
Islamorada.
Tel: (305) 664 0044.
www.casamorada.com

**Little Palm Island Resort
and Spa ★★★★**
The inaccessibility of this
glamorous resort is
actually what draws the
moneyed few, including
a number of former
presidents and foreign

nobility. The property
can only be reached by
seaplane or ferry. Rooms
are spacious and
modern, boasting
ocean views from each
cottage and private
hammocks.
US 1 at Mile Marker 28.5,
Little Torch Key.
Tel: (305) 872 2524.
www.littlepalmisland.com

EATING OUT
Coco's Kitchen ★
Simple dishes served up
with few frills. While
regional Caribbean
and American options
are on the menu, it's
the Cuban specialities
that will make your
mouth water.
283 Key Deer Boulevard,
Big Pine Key.
Tel: (305) 872 4495.
Open: Mon–Sat 7am–
7.30pm.

Butterfly Café ★★★★
Key seafood using only
the best ingredients
available in the area. A
true find.
Tranquility Bay Resort,
2600 Overseas Highway,
Marathon.
Tel: (305) 289 0888.
Open: 7–10am &
11.30am–10pm.

ENTERTAINMENT

Tiki Bar at the Holiday Isle Resort

Nightclub hotspot located directly on the water. Live rock is played nightly from 8.30pm.
US 1 at Mile Marker 84, Islamorada.
Tel: (305) 664 2321.
Open: noon–2am.

SPORT AND LEISURE

Reflections Kayak Nature Tours

The waters of the Keys are shallow and easily navigable, making the chain of islands a great place for novice and advanced sea kayakers. Rentals can be done through Reflections Kayak Nature Tours located at Parmer's Resort (*see p177*).
US 1 at Mile Marker 28.5, Little Torch Key.
Tel: (305) 872 4668.

Key West

ACCOMMODATION

Key West International Hostel and Seashell Motel ★

If you're looking for a cheap room, you can't beat this place. The dorm rooms – popular with backpackers – are a bit dirty and dank. If you can, upgrade to a motel room that comes complete with kitchen.
718 South Street.
Tel: (305) 296 5719.
www.keywesthostel.com

Southernmost Point Guest House ★★

Key West isn't known as a child-friendly destination, yet this affordable guesthouse is a great option if you decide to bring your tots. Located just a block from the beach, the place feels like a bohemian friend's hideaway due to the quirky furnishings.
1327 Duval Street.
Tel: (305) 294 0715. www. southernmostpoint.com

Pier House Resort and Caribbean Spa ★★★★

Location, location, location is what makes this resort one of the finest in Key West. Situated right on Duval Street where it meets the Mallory Docks, the hotel offers unique rooms filled with rich furnishings, some with patios, others with balconies. A great place for a relaxing yet sophisticated holiday.
1 Duval Street.
Tel: (305) 296 4600.
www.pierhouse.com

EATING OUT

El Siboney ★

Fantastic Cuban food at this simple restaurant that's cheap but, oh, so tasty.
900 Catherine Street.
Tel: (305) 296 4184.
Open: Mon–Sat 11am–9.30pm.

Kelly's Caribbean Bar, Grill & Brewery ★★★

Ever wondered what happened to Kelly McGillis of *Top Gun* and *Witness* fame? She opened this fantastic eatery with Caribbean flair.
301 Whitehead Street.
Tel: (305) 293 8484.
www.kellyskeywest.com.
Open: noon–10pm.

ENTERTAINMENT

801 Bourbon Bar/ Number One Saloon

The top gay club in town that's always packed with the male body beautiful and their mates. The drag shows are always hilarious, featuring top female illusionists.

801 Duval Street.
Tel: (305) 296 1992.
Open: 9pm–4am.
Sloppy Joe's
Hemingway's favourite bar and a veritable Key West institution. Regular live music draws a party crowd enticed by both the strong drinks and even stronger literary links.
201 Duval Street.
Tel: (305) 294 5717.
www.sloppyjoes.com.
Open: Mon–Sat 9am–4am, Sun noon–4am.

SPORT AND LEISURE
Fishing
Hemingway was drawn to Key West due to its fishing options, and there are still plenty of them. You'll need a saltwater fishing licence – visit *www.floridaconservation.org* or *tel: (888) 347 4356.*
Swimming
Public beaches are few and far between on Key West, but there are still plenty of sand stretches. Options include **Smathers Beach**, the largest of the lot, which usually draws a loud crowd, **Higgs Beach**, a popular gay beach, and **Fort Zachary Beach**

with its historic fort and ample facilities.

TAMPA AND THE GULF COAST RESORTS
Tampa
ACCOMMODATION
Best Western All Suites Hotel ★
Its location near Busch Gardens and all-suite set-up makes this property the best for families.
3001 University Center Drive. Tel: (813) 971 8930. www. bestwesternflorida.com
Seminole Hard Rock Hotel and Casino ★★
The party place in town for those who want to base themselves in Tampa's action neighbourhood.
5223 Orient Road. Tel: (813) 627 7625. www. hardrockhotelcasinotampa. com

EATING OUT
Mel's Hot Dogs ★
Quintessential hot-dog joint serving up everything from plain dogs to wieners loaded with toppings. Veggie options also available.
4136 E Busch Boulevard. Tel: (813) 985 8000. Open:

Sun–Thur 11am–8pm, Fri & Sat 11am–9pm.
Columbia Restaurant ★★★
Great Spanish and Cuban treats.
2117 7th Avenue. Tel: (813) 248 4961. www. columbiarestaurant.com

ENTERTAINMENT
Seventh Avenue East
Not a club, but an actual street. A club and bar hop along this street between 15th and 20th is a must for those looking for a night of action and adventure.
Bars open: Fri–Sat 9pm–3am.
Tampa Bay Performing Arts Center
This large, multi-stage performing arts centre offers everything from Broadway musicals to opera, theatre to classical concerts.
1010 N MacInnes Place. Tel: (813) 229 7827. www.tampacenter.com

SPORT AND LEISURE
Babe Zaharias Municipal Golf Course
The general public can putt away at this 18-hole course.

11412 Forest Hills Drive.
Tel: (813) 631 4374.
Open: 7am–dusk.

Tampa Bay Buccaneers (American football)
Watch the Buccaneers make their annual Super Bowl challenge at the Raymond James Stadium.
4201 N Dale Mabey Highway.
Tel: (813) 879 2827.
www.buccaneers.com

St Petersburg

ACCOMMODATION

Grayl's Hotel ★
Boutique property situated in a historic Mission-style home.
340 Beach Drive NE.
Tel: (727) 896 1080.
www.graylshotel.com

Ponce de Leon Hotel ★
Better-than-average hotel at a great price. Rooms are quite plain, but are ideal for those who just want a clean room in a good location.
95 Central Avenue.
Tel: (727) 550 9300. www.
poncedeleonhotel.com

EATING OUT

Skyway Jack's ★
Breakfast in America is the stuff dreams are made of. Fluffy pancakes, loaded omelettes, tasty hash browns… and it's all here.
2795 34th Street S.
Tel: (727) 867 1907.
Open: Sun–Thur 11.30am–11pm, Fri–Sat 11.30am–midnight.

Ceviche Tapas Bar and Restaurant ★★
Have as much or as little as you like at this bustling tapas eatery.
95 Central Avenue.
Tel: (727) 209 2302.
www.cevichetapas.com.
Open: Tue–Sat 5pm–2am, Sun 5–10pm.

ENTERTAINMENT

Coliseum Ballroom
Jive your way to happiness at this authentic 1920s ballroom where both young and old dance until dawn.
535 4th Avenue N.
Tel: (727) 892 5202.
Open: hours vary.

SPORT AND LEISURE

Tampa Bay Devil Rays (Baseball)
Watch the Devil Rays in their struggle to make the play-offs.
1 Stadium Drive.
Tel: (727) 825 3137.
http://rays.mlb.com

Clearwater

ACCOMMODATION

Sea Captain Resort ★
Rooms with a tropical feel available for a good price.
40 Devon Drive.
Tel: (727) 446 7550.
www.seacaptainresort.com

Sandpearl Resort ★★
Clearwater's newest resort was completed in summer 2007. The kids' club is a real find, combining both education and active pursuits in its programme.
500 Mandalay Avenue.
Tel: (727) 441 2425.
www.sandpearl.com

EATING OUT

Bobby's Bistro and Wine Bar ★★
Delicious bistro stocked with an incredible wine cellar.
447 Mandalay Avenue.
Tel: (727) 446 9463.
www.bobbysbistro.com

Frenchy's Original Café ★★
Laid-back pub-style eatery that's famous for its filling sandwiches.

41 Baymont Street.
Tel: (727) 446 3607.
www.frenchysonline.com

Entertainment

Palm Pavilion Grill and Bar
Popular live-music venue with bands playing every evening of the week except Mondays.
18 Bay Esplanade.
Tel: (727) 446 6777.
www.palmpavilion.com.
Open: Mon–Fri 10.30am–10pm, Sat & Sun 10.30am–11pm.

Sport and leisure

Clearwater Public Beach
Head down to Clearwater Public Beach for a wide range of activities and facilities including volleyball, fishing on the pier, showers and toilets.
Pier 60.

Sarasota

Accommodation

Best Western Midtown ★
Simple but clean chain hotel that's comfortable enough for the price. Rooms are a little faded around the edges.
1425 S Tamiami Trail.
Tel: (941) 955 9841.
www.bwmidtown.com

Ritz-Carlton Sarasota ★★★
The most exclusive, opulent and newest property in town. Caters to a refined, mature clientele.
1111 Ritz-Carlton Drive.
Tel: (941) 309 2000.
www.ritzcarlton.com

Eating out

Yoder's ★
Pennsylvania Dutch traditions hit the Sunshine State at this down-home Amish restaurant that dishes up country fare.
3434 Bahia Vista Street.
Tel: (941) 955 7771.
www.yodersrestaurant.com

Island Time Grill ★★
Seafood is the speciality of the house at this Caribbean-style restaurant with a well-selected wine list.
8225 Copper Creek Boulevard.
Tel: (941) 351 5128.

Entertainment

Florida State University Center for the Performing Arts
The actual theatre is a 19th-century playhouse that was painstakingly transported to Florida by the Ringling family from Italy back in the 1950s.
5555 N Tamiami Trail.
Tel: (941) 351 8000.
www.asolo.org

Sport and leisure

Sarasota Municipal Golf Course
Practise your swing at the two championship golf courses that make up Sarasota's Municipal Golf Course. Book a tee time at least three days in advance.
1000 Circus Boulevard.
Tel: (941) 365 4653.

Sarasota Polo Club
The sport of kings is played on Sunday afternoons through the winter season.
8201 Polo Club Lane.
Tel: (941) 907 0000.
www.sarasotapolo.com

Fort Myers

Accommodation

Island House Motel ★
Well-located, budget property offering clean, comfortable rooms just a short walk from town.
701 Estero Boulevard.
Tel: (239) 463 9282.

Sanibel Harbour Resort and Spa ★★–★★★

Recently renovated luxury resort boasting views over Sanibel Island, five free-form swimming pools, an award-winning spa and an incredible kids' club.
17260 Harbour Pointe Drive.
Tel: (239) 466 4000.
www.sanibel-resort.com

Eating out
Farmers Market Restaurant ★
Southern restaurant serving up country favourites.
2736 Edison Avenue. Tel: (239) 334 1687. www. farmersmarketrestaurant. com. Open: Mon–Sat 6am–8pm, Sun 6am–7pm.

Morgan House ★★
Enjoy fine cuisine in a casual environment. The kind of place where you can enjoy top-notch dishes while wearing jeans or khakis.
2207 1st Street.
Tel: (239) 337 3377.
Open: Mon–Fri noon–3pm & 7–10pm, Sat 7–10pm.

Entertainment
Barbara B Mann Performing Arts Hall
Fort Myers' premier concert, theatre and live music venue. Everything from jazz to Broadway productions.
8099 College Parkway.
Tel: (239) 481 4849.
www.bbmannpah.com

Sport and leisure
Baseball
Two major-league teams do their spring training in the region: the Boston Red Sox and the Minnesota Twins. The Sox have the stronger following and can be spotted at City of Palms Park.
Edison Avenue at Broadway.
Tel: (239) 334 4799.

Sanibel Island
Accommodation
Palm View Motel ★
The only budget property on Sanibel. Try to splurge for one of the spacious apartments.
706 Donax Street.
Tel: (239) 472 1606.
www.palmviewsanibel.com
Island Inn ★★
In business for over a century, this resort is situated on a wide stretch of Gulf beach and is always packed with repeat clients. Some find it old-fashioned, others a timeless place to experience true Sanibel charm.
3111 W Gulf Drive.
Tel: (239) 472 1561.
www.islandinnsanibel.com

Eating out
Hungry Heron ★
The family restaurant of choice for both islanders and visitors.
Palm Ridge Place, 2330 Palm Ridge Road. Tel: (239) 395 2300. www. hungryheron.com. Open: Mon–Fri 11am–9pm, Sat & Sun 7.30am–9pm.

The Mad Hatter ★★★
The place for a romantic meal. Book early.
6467 Sanibel-Captiva Road. Tel: (239) 472 0033. www.madhatterrestaurant. com. Open: 5–9.30pm.

Entertainment
Old Schoolhouse Theater
Regional theatre performed through the winter season to an appreciative crowd.

1905 Periwinkle Way. Tel: (239) 472 6862. www. oldschoolhousetheater.com

SPORT AND LEISURE
Swimming
Sanibel has plenty of public beaches to choose from, including Turner Beach (for its sunsets), Bowman's Beach (for its seclusion) and Sanibel Lighthouse Beach (for its trails).

Captiva Island
ACCOMMODATION
Captiva Island Inn ★–★★
Cottage-style accommodation in a peaceful location.
11509 Andy Rosse Lane. Tel: (239) 395 0882. www.captivaislandinn.com

EATING OUT
Bubble Room ★
Kitsch eatery packed with 1930s and 1940s trash and treasure. American fare.
15001 Captiva Drive. Tel: (239) 472 5558. Open: noon–10.30pm.
Mucky Duck ★★
Pub grub served up right on the beach.
11546 Andy Rosse Lane. Tel: (239) 472 3434. Open: Mon–Sat

noon–3pm & 7–11pm, Sun noon–3pm.

ENTERTAINMENT
Chadwick's Lounge
Live music and dancing hotspot.
South Seas Island Resort, Captiva Island. Tel: (239) 472 5111. Open: 6pm–midnight.

SPORT AND LEISURE
Captiva Kayak Co.
Rent a kayak or join one of the eco-tours at McCarthy's Marina.
Tel: (239) 395 2925. www.captivakayaks.com

Naples
ACCOMMODATION
Lighthouse Inn Motel ★★
Simple but clean and affordable motel filled with everything you need at a great price.
9140 Gulf Shore Drive N. Tel: (239) 597 3345.
Trianon Old Naples ★★★
Residential property with olde worlde charm.
955 7th Avenue S. Tel: (239) 435 9600. www.trianon.com

EATING OUT
Bistro 821 ★★
This international fusion

eatery feels more South Beach than Old Naples.
821 5th Avenue S. Tel: (239) 261 5821. www.bistro821.com. Open: 5–10pm.
Silver Spoon American Café ★★
Bright and breezy American restaurant that offers high kitsch.
Waterside Shops at Pelican Bay, 5395 N Tamiami Trail. Tel: (239) 591 2123. Open: Sun–Thur 11am– 10pm, Fri & Sat 11am– 11pm.

ENTERTAINMENT
Zoë's
Naples' top nightclub, always filled with the beautiful people.
720 5th Avenue S. Tel: (239) 261 1221. Open: Fri & Sat 10.30pm–2am.

SPORT AND LEISURE
Lely Flamingo (Golf)
Robert Trent Jones Senior designed the championship golf course at Lely Flamingo.
US 41 between Naples and Marco Island. Tel: (239) 793 2223.

THE NORTHEAST

Cape Canaveral and Cocoa Beach

ACCOMMODATION

Hilton Cocoa Beach Oceanfront ★★

This hotel's beachside location is a major plus, but there's a lack of amenities such as patios or balconies on the condo-style rooms.
1550 N Atlantic Avenue.
Tel: (321) 799 0003.
www.hilton.com

The Inn at Cocoa Beach ★★★

Intimate boutique property that feels more like a country home than a beach hotel. Service is personable, suiting the romantic ambience.
4300 Ocean Boulevard.
Tel: (321) 799 3460. www.
theinnatcocoabeach.com

EATING OUT

Rusty's Seafood and Oyster Bar ★–★★★

Relaxed seafood shack next to Port Canaveral pier. Daily happy hour (3–6pm).
628 Glen Creek Drive,
Port Canaveral.
Tel: (321) 783 2033.
www.rustysseafood.com.

Open: Mon–Thur
11am–10pm, Fri–Sat
11am–12.30am, Sun
11am–11pm.

The Mango Tree ★★★★

Elegant surroundings match the imaginative and flavourful continental cuisine.
118 N Atlantic Avenue.
Tel: (321) 799 0513.
Open: Tue–Sun 6–10pm.

ENTERTAINMENT

Cocoa Beach Pier

The bars and venues on the pier host live music on a nightly basis. Places of note include the **Boardwalk Tiki Bar** (at weekends) and **Oh Shuck's Seafood Bar and Grill**.
Meade Avenue at the beach.

SPORT AND LEISURE

Ron Jon Surfing School

Cocoa Beach is Florida's surf capital. The place to go to catch some waves is Cocoa Beach Pier, but don't expect anything like what you might find in Hawaii or California.
150 E Columbia Lane.
Tel: (321) 868 1980.

Daytona Beach

ACCOMMODATION

Shoreline All Suites Inn and Cabana Colony Cottages ★

Small and simple suites with minuscule bathrooms. The whole place feels like a university dorm, albeit much cleaner.
2435 S Atlantic Avenue.
Tel: (386) 252 1692.
www.daytonashoreline.com

The Plaza Resort and Spa ★★

Recently renovated low-rise resort with balconies and all the mod cons. Some rooms even have a Jacuzzi®.
600 N Atlantic Avenue.
Tel: (386) 255 4471. www.
plazaresortandspa.com

The Shores Resort and Spa ★★★

Luxury is the name of the game at this resort. Rooms enjoy sea views and the on-site restaurant is highly recommended.
2637 S Atlantic Avenue.
Tel: (386) 767 7350.
www.shoresresort.com

EATING OUT

The Dancing Avocado Kingdom ★

Most American restaurants cater easily

for vegetarians. This one
specialises in it.
110 S Beach Street.
Tel: (386) 947 2022.
Open: Mon–Sat 8am–4pm.

ENTERTAINMENT
Boot Hill Saloon
Blues bar and honky-
tonk shack catering to
the biker crowd. Always
rowdy yet welcoming.
310 Main Street.
Tel: (386) 258 9506.
Open: noon–1am.

Peabody Auditorium
Look to this venue first
for details on big-name
touring acts.
600 Auditorium Boulevard.
Tel: (386) 254 4545. www.
peabodyauditorium.org

SPORT AND LEISURE
Motor racing
The Daytona International
Speedway is the place to
go for petrolheads. Even if
you can't make the big
race itself, there are usually
stock-car, motorcycle and
go-kart events held on-site
every weekend.
1801 W International
Speedway Boulevard.
Tel: (800) 748 7467.
www.
daytonaintlspeedway.com.
Open: 9am–7pm.

St Augustine
ACCOMMODATION
Casa Monica Hotel ★★
Built in 1888, this fine
hotel is the byword for
luxury in St Augustine.
95 Cordova Street.
Tel: (904) 827 1888.
www.casamonica.com

Monterey Inn ★★
A 1960s-style motel with
simple furnishings.
16 Avenida Menendez.
Tel: (904) 824 4482.

St Francis Inn ★★
The oldest inn in town
dating from 1791,
it still offers all the
conveniences you need.
18 Cordova Street.
Tel: (904) 824 6068.
www.stfrancisinn.com

EATING OUT
**The Bunnery Bakery
and Café ★**
Great place to go for a
light lunch when you
don't want to bust the
bank or the size of
your stomach. A good
choice for coffees and
pastries.
121 St George Street.
Tel: (904) 829 6166.
Open: 8am–6pm.

Gypsy Cab Co ★★★
Every international
cuisine is available at

this laid-back local
favourite.
828 Anastasia Boulevard.
Tel: (904) 824 8244.
www.gypsycab.com. Open:
Mon–Fri 4.30–11pm, Sat
11am–3pm & 4.30–11pm,
Sun 10.30am–3pm.

ENTERTAINMENT
Ann O'Malley's
The latest opening hours
of any pub in town – until
1am daily. Live music.
23 Orange Street.
Tel: (904) 825 4040.
Open: noon–1am.

Scarlett O'Hara's
Live DJs and some
themed karaoke nights
draw the locals to this
19th-century house.
70 Hypolita Street.
Tel: (904) 824 6535.
www.scarlettoharas.net.
Open: Wed–Sun 6pm–
midnight.

SPORT AND LEISURE
Fishing
Cast your rod off the end
of St John's County
Fishing Pier.
Northern tip of St
Augustine Beach.

**Ocean Hammock
Golf Club**
St Augustine's best
course is widely held to

be the Ocean Hammock Golf Club designed by Jack Nicklaus.

Florida A1A between St Augustine and Daytona. Tel: (386) 246 5500. www.oceanhammock.com

Jacksonville

ACCOMMODATION

Hyatt Regency Jacksonville Riverfront ★

Choose the Hyatt if you are doing business in the area or want to be close to Jacksonville's nightlife.

225 E Coast Line Drive. Tel: (904) 354 5080. www.jacksonvillehyatt.com

Riverdale Inn ★

Elegant, period property offering personal service. The on-site restaurant and pub are favourites.

1521 Riverside Avenue. Tel: (904) 354 5080. www.riverdaleinn.com

EATING OUT

BB's ★★★

Wine-bar/bistro with great food.

1019 Hendricks Avenue. Tel: (904) 306 0100. Open: Mon–Thur 11am–10.30pm, Fri 11am–midnight, Sat 10am–midnight, Sun 10am–2pm.

ENTERTAINMENT

Florida Theatre

This 1920s former cinema is now the place to see live acts.

1128 E Forsyth Street. Tel: (904) 355 2787.

San Marco Theatre

Art Deco cinema that gives viewers the chance to order up gourmet sandwiches, pizza, wine and beer.

1996 San Marco Boulevard. Tel: (904) 396 4845. www. sanmarcotheatre.com

SPORT AND LEISURE

AllTel Stadium (American football)

See where the Jaguars play by getting tickets to the AllTel Stadium.

1 AllTel Stadium Place. Tel: (904) 633 6000. www.jaguars.com

Amelia Island

ACCOMMODATION

Hampton Inn and Suites ★★

Wonderful mid-range property that blends in with the historic quarter.

19 S 2nd Street. Tel: (904) 491 4911. www. hamptoninnandsuites.net

Amelia Island Plantation ★★★

There's one word that can be used to describe this property: massive. More like a compound than a resort, the grounds house golf clubhouses, spa centres and a tennis school.

6800 First Coast Highway. Tel: (904) 261 6161. www.aipfl.com

EATING OUT

Marina Restaurant ★★

Amelia Island isn't known for its affordable options. This restaurant breaks the trend by offering country-style cuisine to the masses.

101 Centre Street, Fernandina Beach. Tel: (904) 261 5310. Open: 7–10am & 11.30am–9pm.

Brett's Waterway Café ★★★

The food isn't stunning considering the prices they charge, but the views are amazing.

1 S Front Street. Tel: (904) 261 2660. Open: Mon–Sat 11.30am–2.30pm & 5.30–9.30pm, Sun 5.30–9.30pm.

SPORT AND LEISURE
Kelly Seahorse Ranch (Horse-riding)
Ride on the beach with Kelly Seahorse Ranch.
Amelia Island State Park. Tel: (904) 491 5166. www.kellyranchinc.com

Windward Sailing School
Learn to sail or rent your own boat. If you don't want to be captain, you can even charter a vessel.
Fernandina Harbor Marina, 3977 1st Avenue. Tel: (904) 261 9125.

Orlando
ACCOMMODATION
All-Star Vacation Homes ★★★
Rent a fully furnished townhouse for the price of a three-star room. Nightly and weekly rentals available.
Tel: (407) 997 0733. www.allstarvacationhomes.com

Marriott Grande Vista Resort ★★★
Each unit offers spacious, clean and comfortable accommodation with multiple bedrooms and bathrooms, a living room, laundry, dining area and kitchen. Guests can also use the swimming pools, tennis courts, golf courses, restaurants and other resort amenities.
Tel: (407) 238 7676, (800) 845 5279. www.vacationclub.com

EATING OUT
ESPN Club ★★★
An all-American restaurant and bar where hundreds of TV monitors show a wide range of sporting events. Located along Disney's BoardWalk, guests can also play sports arcade games or participate in trivia contests.
Tel: (407) 939 3463. www.disneyworld.com. Hours vary by season – call for details.

NASCAR Sports Grille ★★★
Racing fans will love dining among the real NASCAR cars on display. American food and a full bar.
Universal CityWalk. Tel: (407) 224 7223. www.nascarsportsgrille.com. Hours vary by season – call for details.

T-Rex ★★★
Life-size animatronic dinosaurs are the main attraction at this prehistoric-themed dining adventure, which serves classic American food such as burgers.
Downtown Disney®. Tel: (407) 827 7777. www.trexcafe.com. Hours vary by season – call for details.

ENTERTAINMENT
Cirque du Soleil: *La Nouba*
Each two-hour show is jam-packed with talented acrobats, aerial artists, cyclists, clowns, performers, musicians, singers and dancers.
Two shows (6pm and 9pm) are presented nightly within a custom-built theatre in the Downtown Disney® area. Tel: (407) 939 1298. www.cirquedusoleil.com

Disney Fishing Excursions
Set off in a chartered boat for a two- or four-hour bass fishing trip. A tour guide and fishing gear are provided.
Tel: (407) 939 7529. Excursions depart daily at 7am, 10am and 1.30pm.

Ice Bar Orlando
This bar is made entirely of ice. There is an admission charge for this

adults-only, 45-minute drinking experience. Cape and gloves provided.
8967 International Drive. Tel: (407) 426 7555. www.icebarorlando.com. Entry times are daily at 7.15pm, 8pm, 8.45pm, 9.30pm, 10.15pm and 11pm. Reservations required.

SPORT AND LEISURE
Faces Skin Care
Over a dozen different facials, performed by certified skincare professionals, are available.
2120 Edgewater Drive. Tel: (407) 426 7690. www.myfacecare.com. Appointment required – call for details.

Shopping
The Mall at the Millenia is one of the largest indoor malls in Florida. It contains hundreds of designer shops, department stores and boutiques.
4200 Conroy Road. Tel: (407) 956 4292. www.mallatmillenia.com. Open: Mon–Sat 10am–9pm, Sun noon–7pm; extended hours during public holidays.

THE PANHANDLE
Tallahassee
ACCOMMODATION
Cabot Lodge North ★
This motel doesn't look like much from the outside, but a closer inspection reveals a few secret charms such as rocking chairs on the porch and a fireplace in the living area.
2735 N Monroe Street. Tel: (850) 386 8880. www.cabotlodgenorthmonroe.com

Doubletree Hotel ★–★★
This hotel is where history was written. Almost all the journalists covering the aftermath of the 2000 elections stayed here.
101 S Adams Street. Tel: (850) 224 5000.

Governor's Inn ★★
Feel like the governor at this elegant hotel.
209 S Adams Street. Tel: (850) 681 6855. www.thegovinn.com

EATING OUT
Bahn Thai ★
Go straight for the spicy Thai delicacies.
1319 S Monroe Street. Tel: (850) 224 4765. Open: Mon–Thur 11am–2.30pm & 5–10pm, Fri 11am–2.30pm & 5–10.30pm, Sat 5–10.30pm.

Chez Pierre ★★★
Tallahassee's upper classes congregate at this French eatery located in a stunning antebellum property.
1215 Thomasville Road. Tel: (850) 222 0936. www.chezpierre.com. Open: Mon–Sat 11am–10pm, Sun 11am–2.30pm & 6–9pm.

ENTERTAINMENT
Floyd's Music Store
Shop and live music venue.
666 W Tennessee Street. Tel: (850) 222 3506. www.floydsmusicstore.com. Open: hours vary.

Tallahassee-Leon County Civic Center
See small-scale touring productions and mid-size live acts perform.
505 W Pensacola Street. Tel: (850) 222 0400. www.tlccc.org

SPORT AND LEISURE
American football
Florida State University's Seminoles are one of the most successful teams in America.

Doak Stadium, Pensacola Street at Stadium Drive. Tel: (850) 644 1830. www.seminoles.com

Biking

Follow the 16-mile (26km) Tallahassee-St Marks Historic Railroad Trail State Park.
Park entrance lies just off the Woodside Highway south of Southeast Capital Circle. www.dep.state.fl. us/gwt/

Panama City

ACCOMMODATION

Beachcomber by the Sea ★★

Rooms have balconies and access to the pool.
17101 Front Beach Road. Tel: (850) 233 3600. www. beachcomberbythesea.com

Marriott's Bay Point Resort Village ★★

Featuring 320 rooms, including 60 golf villas. The tennis and golf facilities are top-notch.
4200 Marriott Drive. Tel: (850) 236 6000. www. marriottbaypoint.com

EATING OUT

Treasure Ship ★–★★★★

This themed venue is a mock Spanish galleon from the 16th century.

On board you'll find everything from small pastry treats through to a five-course meal.
Treasure Island Marina, 3605 S Thomas Drive. Tel: (850) 234 8881. Open: 4.30–10pm.

Shuckums Oyster Pub and Seafood Grill ★★

Everyone comes here for the oysters.
15614 Front Beach Road. Tel: (850) 235 3214. www.shuckums.com

ENTERTAINMENT

Club La Vela

This place calls itself the largest nightclub in America. You'll get lost in rooms of pumping techno.
8813 Thomas Drive. Tel: (850) 234 3866. Open: Thur–Sun 10.30pm–2am.

Schooners

Beach club, live music.
5121 Gulf Drive. Tel: (850) 235 3555. www.schooners.com. Open: 11am–2am.

SPORT AND LEISURE

Shipwreck Island Water Park

Cool off in the lazy river or ride the waves.

12201 Middle Beach Road. Tel: (850) 234 3333. www.shipwreckisland.com. Open: Jun–Jul 10.30am– 5.30pm; Apr–May & Aug–Sept, times vary – call for details.

Pensacola

ACCOMMODATION

Comfort Inn – Pensacola Beach ★

Condo-style property.
40 Fort Pickens Road. Tel: (850) 934 5400. www.comfortinn.com

Hilton Garden Inn ★★★

Beachside property.
12 Via de Luna Drive. Tel: (850) 916 2999. www.hilton.com

EATING OUT

Ever'man Natural Foods ★

Natural food store and deli.
315 W Garden Street. Tel: (850) 438 0402. Open: Mon–Sat 7am– 7pm, Sun 11am–4pm.

ENTERTAINMENT

McGuire's Irish Pub

Lively pub with a brewery on site.
600 E Gregory Street. Tel: (850) 433 6789. Open: 11am–1am.

Index

Acknowledgements

Thomas Cook Publishing wishes to thank JASON CLAMPET for the photographs in this book, to whom the copyright belongs (except for the following images):

WORLD PICTURES/PHOTOSHOT 5, 9, 13, 16, 24, 25, 29, 30, 35, 36, 41, 45, 54, 57, 64, 73, 77, 90, 94, 98, 99, 105, 106, 127, 130, 133, 134, 135, 137, 151, 153, 155, 157, 158, 159, 163, 165, 166; MICHAEL J SCRANTON 59; STIG NYGAARD 95; ROBERT ENGLISH 17, 100, 128; BUSCH GARDENS TAMPA 22, 67; DIANE LEWIS 75, 101; VERSATILE AURE 140; JUDY BAXTER 147; KIP HAVEL 138, 139; MARK A VARGAS 141; DAVID DANZIG 149; J A COULTER 162; WIKIMEDIA COMMONS 44 (JKBrooks 85); 47 (Friejose); 74 (John Bradley); 39, 104, 154 (Infrogmation); 126 (The Gent Family Photos); GEEZERAIR/DREAMSTIME.COM 53; JASON R RICH 1, 70, 107, 108, 109, 110, 111, 112, 118, 119, 120, 121, 122, 123.

For CAMBRIDGE PUBLISHING MANAGEMENT LTD:
Project editor: Karen Beaulah
Copy editor: Anne McGregor
Typesetter: Paul Queripel
Proofreader: Karolin Thomas
Indexer: Karolin Thomas

SEND YOUR THOUGHTS TO
BOOKS@THOMASCOOK.COM

We're committed to providing the very best up-to-date information in our travel guides and constantly strive to make them as useful as they can be. You can help us to improve future editions by letting us have your feedback. If you've made a wonderful discovery on your travels that we don't already feature, if you'd like to inform us about recent changes to anything that we do include, or if you simply want to let us know your thoughts about this guidebook and how we can make it even better – we'd love to hear from you.

Send us ideas, discoveries and recommendations today and then look out for your valuable input in the next edition of this title.

Emails to the above address, or letters to the traveller guides Series Editor, Thomas Cook Publishing, PO Box 227, Coningsby Road, Peterborough PE3 8SB, UK.

Please don't forget to let us know which title your feedback refers to!